S
Pennines

John Gillham

Series Editor:
Terry Marsh

DALESMAN

For Dad

Dalesman Publishing Company
Stable Courtyard, Broughton Hall,
Skipton, North Yorkshire BD23 3AE

First Edition 1996
© John Gillham 1996

A British Library Cataloguing in Publication record
is available for this book

ISBN 1 85568 106 4

Other books in this series:
North Pennines by Alan Hall
(ISBN 1 85568 105 6)

The information given in this book has been provided in good faith and is intended only as a general guide. Whilst all reasonable efforts have been made to ensure that details were correct at the time of publication, the author and Dalesman Publishing Company Ltd cannot accept any responsibility for inaccuracies. It is the responsibility of individuals undertaking outdoor activities to approach the activity with caution and, especially if inexperienced, to do so under appropriate supervision. They should also carry, and be capable of using properly, the appropriate equipment and maps, be properly clothed and have adequate footwear. The sport described in this book is strenuous and individuals should ensure that they are suitably fit before embarking upon it.

Contents

INTRODUCTION

Lying between the Yorkshire Dales and the Peak District National Parks, the South Pennines are the forgotten hills of Northern England, but these moors, which lie virtually in the backyards of several million people, have a dramatic aura all of their own.

Many walkers' first experience of the South Pennines is on the Pennine Way, which hereabouts follows the watershed from Marsden Moor to Stoodley Pike. They will remember the wide expanses of heather and cotton-grass, the gritstone cliffs and tors and the dusky mill villages that squeeze into the tight, wooded valleys; they may remember the wild flowers that grow profusely in the meadows, the drystone walls and the quaint 17th-century farmhouses with mullioned windows. Yet there is much more.

This is wonderful walking country where history is ingrained on every pasture, from the earthworks of a Roman fort to the crumbling farmstead high on the hill. All have a special story to tell. The old paved path that straddles the moor would, before the coming of the railways, be buzzing with long packhorse trains carrying salt, coal and limestone across the country. Hidden by thick woodland in some dale head there may be the remains of an old mill, once thriving, before the days of steam took the workforce down into the valleys. It may be remote now, but that reservoir would have been hewn from the hillside by a thousand navvies, who would have lived in an adjacent long-forgotten shanty town. The path to it may have been the trackbed of an old steam railway built to carry rock for the dam – the tell-tale signs are usually there to be found.

Dramatic scenery breeds dramatic people: many famous writers, and poets, including the Brontë sisters, Edmund

Spenser, and Poet Laureate, Ted Hughes, lived in and loved these parts.

From the northern outliers of Ilkley Moor and Pendle Hill to the Saddleworth Edges in the south, millstone grit takes a strong hold, its dark and rugged outlines adding drama to the hills.

The Pennine ridge formed over millions of years in a great upheaval of the rocks known by geologists as an anticline. The Pennine Anticline is believed to have reached 13,000ft/ 4,000m above sea level, but, gradually the softer shales, coal measures and limestones were eroded from the tops and washed into the sea leaving the harder millstone grits on the surface. Similar anticlines were formed at Rossendale, Pendle and Lothersdale.

Later, glaciation played a large part in shaping deep valleys such as the Cliviger Gorge and Yorkshire's Calder. The glaciers also scoured boulders of limestone from the Ribblesdale and Craven areas and carried them into the South Pennines. The remains of old limestone quarries or hushings can still be seen in the Thursden valley and Worsthorne Moor.

Perhaps the best known and most spectacular peak is Pendle Hill, a dark giant amid the emerald plains of East Lancashire and the Ribble valley. In the days before accurate instruments measured the land, Pendle was believed to be over 4,000ft (1,200m). It has since been adjusted to 1,830ft (557m).

Facing Pendle across Nelson and Burnley, Boulsworth Hill, was until recently out of bounds. Now, the walker can climb to its rocky summit using a permissive path, one of many negotiated by various councils and landowners in the region.

Calderdale is the richest gem among the South Pennines. Here the moors are penetrated by deep, crag-fringed valleys, lush with oak, ash and birch woodland and enlivened by rushing streams. On the way to the tops, the well-maintained paths climb to historical hilltop weaving villages where cottages, cafes and inns cluster round cobbled streets.

South of Calderdale, the Pennines narrow to be crowded by the industrial suburbs of West Yorkshire and Greater Manchester. The hills themselves are not diminished; in fact the ridge is more pronounced. Many ancient highways and byways, including the Blackstone Edge Roman road, offer splendid circular routes to the summits, where the celebrated landmarks of the city can be surveyed in peace and under the widest skies in the North.

PUBLIC TRANSPORT

Public transport in the South Pennines is as extensive as anywhere in England. Thanks to some good planning and West Yorkshire's Metro system, in which bus and rail links are co-ordinated, it is possible to get regular transport to some remote corners of the region. The Metro Day Rover offers unlimited travel within the county on buses and trains (leaflets are available from the tourist information centres – see Useful Addresses, or ring the Metro Travel Information Service: 0113 245 7676).

I have listed the available transport (at the time of writing) that could be used on the linear walks, which would otherwise require the use of two cars, and on walks starting from remote places.

EQUIPMENT AND SAFETY

It is extremely important that all hillwalkers are fully equipped and practised in the use of map and compass. Their well-being may depend on it one day. When the mist comes down on the hills it is essential to know exactly where one is and the direction required to get safely off the mountain.

Make sure to take enough food and water – keep additional emergency rations in the corner of the rucksack. Not taking enough food is the quickest way of becoming tired, and being tired is the quickest way of sustaining an injury.

Good waterproofs are essential. Remember, getting cold and wet will render the walker vulnerable to hypothermia, even outside the winter months. Modern breathable fabrics, such as those made with Gore-Tex, Cyclone and Sympatex linings, are generally regarded as the best. Some walkers, however, prefer to go for the non-breathable types, which are cheaper, lighter and more compact. Unfortunately, the condensation that forms on the inside of the garments makes the wearer feel wet and uncomfortable when they are taken off.

It is important to wear good walking boots on the hills, for shoes have insufficient grip and ankle support on difficult terrain. Even the lower-level walks can become slippery after rainfall. Many an ankle has been twisted or leg broken for the lack of proper footwear.

When snow and ice cover the hills it is more prudent to be equipped with, and know how to use, crampons and an ice-axe. Keep the latter out, once on the slopes, for an ice-axe strapped to a rucksack never saved anyone.

It is a good idea to pack some emergency medical supplies (plasters bandages etc.): there are plenty of good kits available.

MAPS
While the maps accompanying each walk are beautifully

crafted they are not detailed enough for use in the field. Pathfinder and Outdoor Leisure 1:25000 maps are best as they show greater detail including the important field boundaries. The double-sided Ordnance Survey® Outdoor Leisure Map of the South Pennines covers most of the walks in the book. Only where a walk is outside the area covered by this map, are map details given in the information section at the start of the walk.

The Pathfinder Sheets 671 (SE04/14) and 682 (SE03/13) cover the walks on Ilkley Moor. Pathfinder Sheets 669 and 680 complete the Clitheroe Castle and Spence Moor walks, and the OS Outdoor Leisure Dark Peak map covers the Saddleworth Edges route.

Alternatively, you can use OS Landranger (1:50 000) sheets 103, 104, 109 and 110.

ACCESS
The South Pennines have a vast network of footpaths largely due to the old industries. Many are old routes used by miners and mill workers. Others are ancient roads and packhorse trails. In addition, the water companies have created several access areas and many miles of new permissive routes through their moorlands and around their reservoirs. Some of the heather moors, like those east of Boulsworth Hill, are managed for grouse-shooting. If you are on a public right of way you have the right to be there at ALL times, but walkers are not usually welcome to roam off the line of the path. These areas are particularly sensitive during the nesting times (April and May) and on shoots (August 12 to December 12).

CARING FOR THE COUNTRYSIDE
With modern methods and increased productivity for the large units, it is becoming much harder for farmers to make a living from the land. Walkers can help by showing

consideration for the rural environment, which means shutting gates behind them (except for those that are wedged open), not leaving litter, and by keeping dogs on a lead in sheep country.

Unfortunately, the explosion of people taking to the hills has meant that the footpaths have become eroded. Tom Stephenson's long green trail (the Pennine Way) has been so deeply grooved into the hillsides that various authorities have deemed it necessary to inlay the route with heavy gritstone slabs. There is not a lot the walker can do (except the unthinkable, staying at home) but they can help in a small way:

Avoid walking in very large groups.

Do not walk along the very edge of the footpath, which makes it wider.

If a cart track has one of those pleasant grass islands through the middle, keep it that way by sticking to the stony bits.

Do not wear heavyweight mountain boots for low-level or moorland paths. Use a lightweight pair if possible.

Walk single file across farming land.

USEFUL ADDRESSES

Tourist Information Centres:
Barnoldswick: The Old Library, Fernlea Avenue.
    Tel: 01282 817046
Burnley: Burnley Mechanics, Manchester Road.
    Tel: 01282 455485
Halifax: Piece Hall.
    Tel: 01422 368725
Haworth: 2-4 West Lane.
    Tel: 01535 642329
Hebden Bridge: 1 Bridge Gate.
    Tel: 01422 843831
Ilkley: Station Road.
    Tel: 01943 602319
Nelson: Town Hall, Market Street.
    Tel: 01282 692890
Rochdale: The Clock Tower, Town Hall.
    Tel: 01706 356592
Skipton: 9 Sheep Street.
    Tel: 01756 792309
Todmorden: 15 Burnley Road.
    Tel: 01706 818181

The Calderdale Countryside Service: Wellesley Park,
Halifax.
    Tel: 01422 359454
The Ramblers' Association: 1-5 Wandsworth Road,
London. SW8 2XX
    Tel: 0171 582 6878

Location Map

The numbers on this location map roughly indicate the starting point of each of the walks in the book.

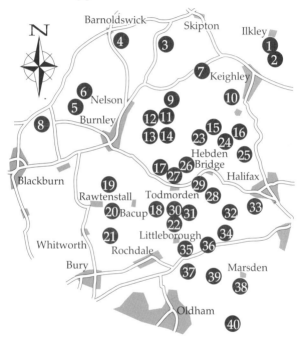

THE NORTHERN HILLS

The northern region of the South Pennines includes some of its finest and most diverse scenery. Pride of place must go to Pendle Hill, that dark escarpment rising from the banks of the Ribble and Lancashire Calder to what the locals proudly call its Big End, overlooking Barley. This fine hill, with its roots steeped in witchcraft and sorcery, separates the attractive rural aspects of the Ribble valley and the more severe industrial townscapes of East Lancashire.

In the shadow of Pendle's northern slopes is Clitheroe, a fine town clustered around the keep of its Norman castle. One of the best walks in the area combines Clitheroe with the historical abbey village of Whalley, taking in the sullen north-eastern slopes of Pendle Hill for good measure.

Anyone looking east from Pendle's summit will realise that there is more to the area than just one hill, for spread out between here and the Aire valley is a pleasing complex of little hills – less wild, but more verdant and with fine natural sculpturing.

Two of them, Weets Hill and Pinhaw Beacon, offer wonderful circular routes that explore tree-lined river and canal banks and saunter through flower-filled meadows. Pinhaw Beacon, which many Pennine Way-farers will remember, has a thick carpet of heather and spectacular views north to the peaks of the Yorkshire Dales.

Earl Crag, the last bony knuckle of Ickornshaw's heather moors, lies to the south-east. Crowned by two monuments, Lund's Tower and Wainman's Pinnacle, it dominates the landscape for many a mile and looks down on Cowling, *an industrial village in the heart of verdant countryside between Colne and Keighley. Again it is well known by Pennine Way walkers, who see its bold outlines from afar as they descend pastureland to the west.*

Ilkley Moor makes one last stand for the South Pennines, its gritstone crags staring defiantly across the River Wharfe to the Yorkshire Dales. It is a bold moor that shelters the affluent country town of Ilkley from the west winds and also shuts out sight and sounds of industrial Airedale. Popular both with walkers and climbers, its prominent crags and bluffs jut out from carpets woven from bracken and heather, studded with rowan and pine. Colour comes to Ilkley like a chameleon, changing with sunlight and season. This is a fine place to start or end a discovery of the South Pennine hills.

1 Ilkley Moor

Ilkley Moor, the most northerly outpost of the South Pennines, dips its feet in the Wharfe, that most noble of Yorkshire dales. This is popular walking country, where the moorland heights are lined with crags of sandstone and gritstone, some inscribed with ancient markings. This circular walk traces the Wharfe's riverbanks before climbing to the craggy moorland edge.

Distance:
8 miles/13km

Height gain:
1,150ft/350m

Walking time:
5 hours

Start/Finish:
Castle Street, by the Wharfe road bridge, Ilkley. GR118479.

Type of walk:
A combination of riverside and field paths, and well-defined moorland tracks.

Map:
OS Pathfinder Sheet 671 (SE04/14). Roadside car parking.

Ilkley sits snugly by the banks of the Wharfe showing a pleasant and affluent face to the world.

The Romans built their fort Olicana here in AD79, but the town gained impetus when the Victorians rediscovered its healthy spa waters. Broad tree-lined streets, landscaped gardens and hillside mansions all date back to those halcyon days.

Today, Ilkley is a busy little town catering for tourists and walkers. It is the starting point of the Dales Way, a popular long distance route across the Yorkshire Dales to the Lake District at Bowness.

Take the path from Castle Street towards the banks of the Wharfe where a Tarmac path, part of the Dales Way, follows the riverside west beneath the road bridge and through parkland. It passes a fine three-arched footbridge, crosses a road and continues close to the river between a nursery and some houses. By a sports field the route follows a Tarmac drive to the clubhouse where a Dales Way (DW) sign points the way west across fields. Several kissing gates line the route, which re-acquaints itself with the wide, swift-flowing Wharfe near a sub-station, enshrouded with trees and shrubs.

Turn left and leave the Dales Way by The Hollins (GR098483 – not named on Landranger maps), following a fenced path to the A65. The path across the road is staggered slightly to the left. Once over the step stile in the fence, turn right along the bottom edge of the field and go through a five-bar gate. Head south-west to the top right hand corner of the next field and go through a gap stile that lies just beyond a small dyke. Trace the fence on the left for a short way, then go through another gap stile, aiming for the top right of the field – a farm road will be crossed en route. Follow the top edge of the next two fields, cross a farm road, and continue west and to the left of a small Leylandii plantation to reach a farming hamlet, marked Netherwood House on the map.

Follow the drive through the hamlet. Go through the gate to the left of the last house, Rams Gill Cottage, and climb across another field, to a gap stile in the wall on the right. Beyond it the path follows the top of the field and goes through another stile on the left. By now the climb is steeper and there are good views to Blubberhouses Moor, which soars from the park-like fields of Wharfedale.

Head for the gap stile at the top right corner of the field and continue south-west to meet a farm road, which should be followed as it arcs to the right through a five-bar gate towards Crag House. Leave the track and go through a gate in the field's top wall, turning right along a cart track. At the field corner by Crag House (GR083475), turn left to climb to the hill-side. A deeply grooved track develops and takes the route to the edge of the moor. Climb the steps to the gap stile in the tall drystone wall and follow a track raking left up the bracken-clad hillside. The path soon becomes a wide stony track, which gains the northern "edge" route. Follow this east with fine views opening up over Ilkley.

Many crags line the route but the most interesting hereabouts is the Swastika Stone, a huge boulder protected from vandalism by railings and engraved with the Indo-European sign of eternity. The carving is believed to have Bronze Age origins.

Beyond the Swastika Stone the path descends slightly to run along the top edge of a small reservoir. It is now a well-used stony path that runs along the back of some very salubrious housing to join a narrow Tarmac lane. Descend along the lane for 50yds/m, then turn right on a narrow path that squeezes through two gorse bushes and climbs to White Wells.

In the mid-18th century, Squire Middleton used the charming whitewashed cottage as a cold water bath cure centre. Today the cottage is a museum/visitor centre and exhibits the old stone plunge pool.

Turn right by the cottage on a stony track climbing the hillsides, which are fringed by the cliffs of Ilkley Crag. Although it is feasible for the high ridge to be gained at Lanshaw Lad, this route leaves the track for a good path to the left, heading east beneath the cliffs to cross Backstone Beck.

There is a profusion of paths and tracks in this vicinity – some are old quarrying routes while others are eroded shortcuts that reflect the high level of use to which these moors are subjected.

Take the prominent path that descends north-east to

skirt some quarries fringed by pine trees. It then descends over the rim of the moor beneath the Cow and Calf, the Cow being a 100ft/30m buttress that over-looks the Calf, a gigantic boulder.

After passing a car park the path crosses the road and descends west of a golf course on a sunken grassy path. Keep the wall to the right as the path enters scrubby woodland to meet the road at Ben Rhydding, south-east of Ilkley.

Head north on the road, going past the Wheatley pub and beneath the railway, then turn left along the A65. A footpath opposite the Hollygarth pub leads to the Wharfe's riverbanks. Follow the riverside path west for 1.3 miles/2km to the start of the walk.

2 Ilkley to Saltaire

This linear station-to-station walk includes the popular classic over Ilkley Moor to Dick Hudson's pub, combining it with a descent of Shipley Glen to Saltaire. The fine Model Village makes a fascinating finishing point for those interested in architecture and history.

Distance:
7 miles/11km

Height gain:
935ft/285m

Walking time:
4 hours

Start:
Ilkley Railway Station or nearby car park. GR118476.

Finish:
Saltaire Railway Station, or nearby car park off Victoria Street. GR139382.

Type of walk:
Moorland paths followed by farm tracks, field paths and parks.

Maps:
OS Pathfinder Sheets 671 (04/14) and 682 (03/13) or Landranger 104.

Public Transport:
By rail: Saltaire is on the Skipton to Leeds/ Bradford line. To get back to Ilkley change at Keighley. Buses take a similar route.

From the railway station head south on Wells Promenade and keep south on the well-worn path climbing Ilkley Moor to White Wells.

In the mid-18th century, Squire Middleton used this charming whitewashed cottage as a cold water bath cure centre. Today, it is a museum/visitor centre and exhibits the old stone plunge pool.

A stony track climbs further, veering south-east towards Ilkley Crags. Ignore the left fork, which skirts the foot of the crags in a little depression known as Rocky valley. Instead, keep on the track straddling the moor to the left.

Rocky valley was caused by a landslip between the shale and gritstone strata during the last Ice Age. Views back across tree-studded Wharfedale and Ilkley include the buff-tinted moors of Denton, Middleton and Blubberhouses. Ahead, Ilkley Moor gradually swells to the skyline in a windswept expanse of short-cropped heather and moor grasses.

The wide path traverses the moor, fording a little stream, Backstone Beck, at Gill Head. It continues to the Twelve Apostles, a stone circle marking a Bronze Age burial tumulus.

Views from here show a wide slice of urban Yorkshire, including Leeds, Guiseley, Otley and the white golf balls of the early warning station on Menwith Hill, but they also encompass attractive expanses of rolling hillside paling into the mist of the horizon.

Beyond the Apostles the path straddles the ridge, squeezes through a stile in a moorland wall and descends south across Bingley Moor.

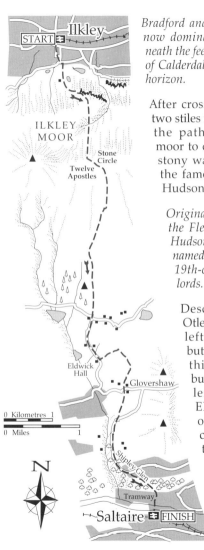

Bradford and its satellites now dominate views beneath the feet, but the hills of Calderdale decorate the horizon.

After crossing another two stiles in crosswalls, the path leaves the moor to descend on a stony walled path to the famous old Dick Hudson pub.

Originally known as the Fleece, the Dick Hudson pub was renamed after one of its 19th-century landlords.

Descend on the Otley Road to the left of the pub but take care on this narrow busy lane. Turn left opposite Eldwick Hall on to an enclosed farm track.

When it ends continue through a five-bar gate and

across fields, keeping the top wall to the left. Turn right by a prominent wall corner following a fence (not marked on the map). The path leads through two more gates then turns half right on a track to Golcar Farm. Pass to the left of the farmyard and across a step stile then turn right along a grassy track passing to the south of the house. This leads to a drive that continues to the road opposite Glovershaw Farm.

Immediately opposite, a narrow footpath (signposted "To the Glen"), squeezes between holly bushes to the right of a barn. It follows the western banks of a dyke, Glovershaw Beck, whose little depression deepens to become a wooded dene. The path climbs out to a quarry, where suddenly there is activity of the human kind. Most Sundays there are hikers, bikers and picnickers in abundance all creating a confusing network of paths. Fortunately, all go to the nearby road.

The best of the paths keeps to the right of the quarries. On meeting the road keep to the right then follow a path on the rocky edge of the dene, which is now known as Shipley Glen. As the path bends to the left the Airedale towns of Bingley and Shipley come into view.

The path finally rejoins the road by the Old Glen House pub. Follow the road passed some houses to the top station of the Shipley Glen Tramway.

The rope-hauled passenger tramway, which was built in 1895 by Samuel Wilson, descends to Roberts Park in the valley. (Open to visitors on Saturday afternoons and Sundays between Easter and October, and Wednesdays during June and July.)

For the walker, a Tarmac path descends by the tramway and by a sports field to the road. Go into the park opposite and cross the footbridge over the River Aire into impressive Saltaire.

Titus Salt, a wealthy mill owner and then Mayor of Bradford, who had been saddened by the city's industrial troubles and pollution, decided to move his mills into one unit. This would be built in a cleaner environment and would be part of a newly constructed Model Village. After finding his site at Shipley in the Aire valley, Salt employed the best architects to design his project – Saltaire.

The village comprises 22 streets (named after Salt's wife, children and other family members), 850 beautifully-constructed houses in an area of 25 acres. Particularly notable are the beautiful Congregational Church, the six-storey mill itself, which was built in Venetian style, and the Public Hall.

The path continues to the towpath of the Leeds and Liverpool Canal, where there is a spasmodic waterbus service to Shipley. Turn left on to the main road by the mill, then right down Victoria Street to the railway station or car park.

3 Pinhaw Beacon

Pinhaw Beacon watches over the pleasant pastureland of Elslack and the Aire valley, and keeps the secret of Lothersdale from the outside world. Its trig point caps a high ridge of well-nurtured heather – a mantle of purple-pink amid all that green. Pinhaw can be visited from a high roadside car park, but to conquer this hill in a way it truly deserves, the best route is from the valley at Thornton-in-Craven.

Distance:
8 miles/13km

Height gain:
1,210ft/370m

Walking time:
4 hours

Start/Finish:
Thornton-in-Craven.
GR908486. Roadside
car parking on Old
Lane.

Type of walk:
A largely pastoral walk with a steady climb to the heather moors of the Beacon and some forestry paths and tracks on the return route.

Descend on Old Lane past the charming cottages and under an old railway bridge. From here the tree-lined

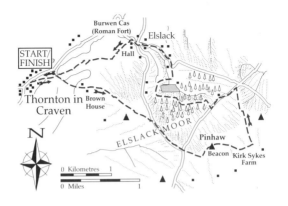

lane climbs to Brown House Farm. Abandon the Tarmac beyond the farmhouse and climb the stile to the left. The path traverses a very mucky corner of the field before climbing west to cross a little dyke on a plank bridge. Turn right beyond the adjacent stile and climb the rising fields by the fence. The dyke becomes deeper set in a clough filled with rowan, hawthorn and elder. The map marks a large coppice here, but it is something of an exaggeration.

After going through a gated gap stile by a five-bar gate the path kinks with the wall to the right before resuming its course parallel to the now shallowing clough. A Pennine Way sign directs the route across a footbridge over the stream and then uphill to the left, where some boardwalks over marshy ground remind the walker that this is Tom Stephenson's long green trail.

After climbing a ladder stile in a particularly tall stone wall the terrain becomes rougher: there has been a change from pasture to rushy moorland. The heather of Elslack Moor comes into view on the skyline, as does the radar mast on Proctor's Height.

The path joins a narrow Tarmac lane to a T-junction high on the moor. Go straight ahead on a sunken track that swings left to the trig point on Pinhaw Beacon's summit.

What a view! Across the plains of the Aire and the Ribble North Yorkshire's peaks parade themselves across the horizon, from majestic Ingleborough's two-tiered massif on the left to the dark crags of Barden Moor on the right. To the south, the countryside is rolling and verdant with the twin monuments of Earl Crag standing proud of the swelling heather fields of Ickornshaw Moor.

The cairned track continues across the heathery ridge, veering east-south-east down Little Pinhaw. As it converges with a stone wall it degenerates into a narrower path through the moor grass and rushes that have merged with the heather. The little valley of Lothersdale has been revealing its secrets gradually, but now the village is in full view amid a complex of emerald fields. Turn right, still following the wall, and cross the stile with Kirk Sykes Farm directly ahead.

Locals will often tell the tale of Swine Harry when Pinhaw comes into the conversation. The poor man stole a pig and made his escape across the moor at night. In order to climb the stile, he looped the pig's lead around his neck to leave both hands free. Unfortunately, he stumbled at the top of the stile. Next morning a local farmer found him strangled by the weight of the beast, which dangled on the opposite side.

Leave the Pennine Way, which descends into Lothersdale. Instead, turn left by the wall to a primitive stile and pick up the footpath doubling back over the heather moors (GR955472). The footpath is little more than a sheep track, close to the wall.

On Ransable Hill those views return. This time Skipton is added to the scene, nestling in the plains between Rombalds Moor and Barden Moor.

Beyond a stile in the moor's perimeter wall, the path emerges on the road by a cattle grid to the south of the Standrise plantation. Turn left along the road then right along a signposted footpath through the forest. It begins as a wonderful little path over a bed of pine needles but, on crossing the first track, it degenerates into a scruffy course through a forest ride. Yellow arrows help route finding.

The path turns half left along a stony track; the stones are in fact the remains of the drystone wall marked on the map. Go straight ahead at the crossroads (GR942482) on a wide dirt road that veers right. The footpath waymarkers do not highlight the path's next turn by a broken down wall (GR938481), but the path does exist.

Turn right by the wall to a single gatepost, then go through the gap to its left side. From here a grassy path descends to a rutted forestry path not far from the shores of Elslack Reservoir. Go left along the track to meet the dirt road, recently abandoned. Now stony, the route descends to the reservoir's dam and crosses the outflow. The overflow rarely has water in it, but can be icy in winter.

Follow the track as it turns right along the northern shores. Stay with it to the end where it swings left descending past Storles House Farm and on to Moor Lane. This winding Tarmac road, lined by hedges of holly, wild rose, bramble and beech, descends splendidly into Elslack, a tiny hamlet with pretty stone-built cottages surrounding a small green.

Go over a dilapidated stile by a barn on a signposted footpath along the field edge. Two adjacent stiles to the left show the way past a cowshed and on to a cart track heading south-west through fields. The 14th-century Elslack Hall peeps out from behind the farm buildings.

The earthwork remains of the Elslack Roman fort lie to the north, bisected by the disused railway that used to link Skipton and Colne. This would once have been busy with Roman legionnaires on the road between Ribchester and Ilkley.

Leave the cart track at a five-bar gate in the fence to the right (GR925490), and climb over the hill in the field to descend to a stile at its far end. Continue diagonally across the next field and cross the bridge over the old railway trackbed. Once across turn left past a stone-built barn. The path stays parallel to the old railway and a line of trees, but gradually it descends to cross a stream on a wooden footbridge that remains hidden by bushes until the last moment. An overgrown path continues through scrub to join the outward route on the Brown House Farm approach road. Turn right along it and under the railway bridge to return to Thornton.

4 Weets Hill

Weets Hill may be nowhere near the highest top in the South Pennines, but it does offer some of the best views. A proliferation of well-maintained footpaths also allows a really good itinerary to be plotted, here blending an interesting mix of canal towpath, lakeshore and hill. Choose a bright day in early summer for this one: the meadows will be glowing with the colour of wild flowers and those cow-trodden field corners should have dried out.

Distance:
9 miles/15km

Height gain:
820ft/250m

Walking time:
4-5 hours

Start/Finish:
Salterforth Wharf, near Barnoldswick. GR887454. Good-sized free car park.

Type of walk:
A fairly easy walk with a moderate climb to Weets Hill. A good combination of farm paths across fields, a little moorland and some easy level walking on the canal towpath.

In an idyllic lazy start to the walk, amble north along the towpath and under the Barnoldswick road. It is short but sweet, as the canal must be forsaken by

Cockshot Bridge (GR886463), which lies just beyond the abutments of the old railway bridge. Leave the towpath and turn left across the bridge on a track that cuts across fields. A left turn along a lane leads to the main road. The on-going path is staggered 50yds/m to the left, initially on an unsignposted Tarmac drive by a large house called Parklands, then on a rutted track climbing the pastures of Higher Park.

At the top of the field go through the left of two gates and maintain a south-westerly direction to a farm lane passing the aptly named Bleak House. Turn right along the country lane, then take the left fork, passing Bancroft Mill.

Built in 1922, Bancroft Mill was the last cotton-weaving mill to be constructed in Barnoldswick. It was closed and largely demolished in 1978, but its engine house and chimney remain as a museum, open to the public during the summer.

Turn left into Moorgate Road, a short avenue of modern housing. This leads to a pleasant country road known a Folly Lane, which climbs a pastoral spur thrown out by Weets Hill. Elder, holly, bramble, hawthorn and a myriad varieties of wild flower border the lane. In early summer the meadows will be splashed with the vivid yellow of buttercups. Watch out for the Pendle Way sign (a witch on a broomstick). It highlights the little stile in the wall to the right, which must be scaled to gain access to a delightful path climbing west over high pastures at the spur's edge.

By now there are good views, both back over Barnoldswick and north to Bowland and the Three Peaks – Ingleborough, Whernside and Pen y Ghent.

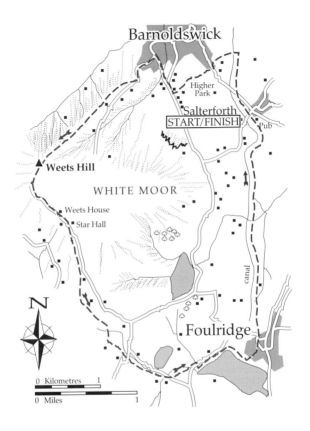

The path becomes a more prominent track with the rock bed close to the surface and surrounded by rushes. It passes through an area that was obviously quarried in times past, but which is now well cloaked with grass. Near the top of Weets Hill, a right fork climbs past a stone-built cairn to the summit trig point.

The views have now reached panoramic proportions. Pendle

Hill is added to the scene, overwhelming the neighbouring rolling hills. To its left stands a small castellated tower. This is Blacko Tower, a folly built around 1890 for Jonathan Stansfield who mistakenly believed he would be able to see into Ribblesdale from its viewing platform. He took his disappointment philosophically, saying "I have never drunk nor smoked in my life, so am making this as my hobby".

A well-used track heads back to the main right of way by the stone wall. It passes to the left of Weets Hill Farm to the terminus of a Tarmac lane, the Gisburn Old Road. This descends past a couple of cottages and the rather grandly named Star Hall. Another Pendle Way sign points the way across more meadows, skewing away slightly from the road by a stone wall that slightly obscures the view down to the green and pleasant valley to the right.

The path switches to the other side of the wall just before reaching a walled track that crosses the route. The Pendle Way proper turns right and down into the valley from here, but maintain direction, following the wall for about 300yds/m.

Skilfully-concealed steps in the wall by a small copse mark the start of the route down to Foulridge, whose reservoirs bask amid green fields framed by the buff moors of Boulsworth and Ickornshaw. On Sunday afternoons, the lower reservoir will be buzzing with sailing dinghies scudding across its waters.

A wall acts as a guide for the first part of the descent. When it veers right, maintain direction to the bottom right-hand corner of the field where there is a primitive stile. Turn right and follow the wall at the top edge of the hay field. In summer, before the crop is cut, the field may be thick with wild flowers and tall grasses of many colours and varieties.

On meeting a path from the right (Malkin Tower Farm) veer left for the bottom corner of the field. The path passes to the left of a row of whitewashed terraced cottages to meet a lane west of the Slipper Hill Reservoir. On the opposite side of the road a signposted path follows the left field edge and squeezes between two cottages back to the road close to the reservoir dam. Turn right along the road to reach a stony track just beyond the course of an old railway. Marked by another Pendle Way white arrow, the tree-lined track heads north-east directly towards the Foulridge Lower Reservoir, whose dam and sailing clubhouse lie just across a lane. A path along the northern shores begins from the back of the car park.

Foulridge Lower is a pleasantly-set reservoir surrounded by low green hills and rich foliage. Yachtsmen, fishermen and mallards co-exist and its barren man-made shoreline of boulders is often tempered by the cover of rushes and scrub.

After rounding to the north-eastern shores past some very opulent housing, a dusky little ginnel climbs to one of Foulridge's newer housing estates. Keep north to Sycamore Rise, and there turn right. Turn left on reaching the B-road and follow the signs for Foulridge Wharf down Warehouse Road to reach the towpath of the Leeds-Liverpool Canal. There is a tea shop here for the thirsty.

The two miles of towpath back to Salterforth Wharf are a delightfully easy way to end the walk. Shaded by an unending avenue of trees, the canal passes through wonderful rural scenery; the moors of Kelbrook and Bleara topping the verdant plains to the east with the more intimate pastured knolls rising from the western banks. It is all rather like one of those pastoral scenes from a butter advert.

5 Pendle Hill

Soaring from the chequered plains of the Ribble valley and the industrial spread of East Lancashire, the whaleback of Pendle Hill dominates the scenery for many a mile. The hill has been synonymous with tales of witchcraft since the famous trials of Demdike, Chattox and their clans at Lancaster, when nineteen poor souls were found guilty and put to death. This exploratory walk discovers most aspects of the hill, and strides along its two steepest edges to eke out the best views of distant landscapes.

Distance:
7 miles/11km

Height gain:
1,115ft/340m

Walking time:
4 hours

Start/Finish:
Car park and picnic site
at Barley. GR823403.

Type of walk:
A moderate circular
walk over moorland.

**Not recommended in
misty conditions.**

Turn right out of the car park and along the road to its junction with the road from Newchurch.

Immediately opposite, a metalled cul-de-sac (signposted "Barley Green"), takes the route through a cluster of cottages, leading to a cart track, which climbs west, passing the northern shores of the larger of Ogden's two reservoirs. Pendle Hill's steep eastern face, known affectionately as the Big End, looms large in views ahead. The wide track climbs to the right of Upper Ogden Reservoir's dam, where a path begins, beyond a stone step stile. It heads west above the upper reservoir and over two stiles to enter Ogden Clough.

Hill slopes of grass and bracken enclose the stream, which dashes over a rocky bed. They gradually close in to form a tight ravine, shutting out the rest of the world. After crossing a side stream, the route climbs over rocky slopes to a wooden barrier and a Pendle Way sign at the edge of a large tract of bracken. Here a path continues along the northern slopes of the clough. Ignore the next Pendle Way sign pointing up the hill and maintain direction on a narrow path, little more than a sheeptrack in places. After traversing patches of bracken the path descends to ford the stream, which now arcs north. A faint path climbs a grassy ramp on the opposite bank to a better one that traces the rim of the clough. This, in turn, meets a prominent and well-used track from the Nick of Pendle, leading over rough peaty ground above the clough.

Abandon the path at GR790404, to follow the course of an old wall north-west across Turn Head. At an intersection of walls close to the northern edge of the moor, turn right to pick up a path that rounds Mearley Clough to climb to Scout Cairn, a huge pile of stones commemorating 75 years of scouting, from where the views are especially outstanding.

The clear grassy path continues at the escarpment's edge and parallel to a tall stone wall that runs along the crest of the ridge. On reaching a ladder stile in the wall, the route turns right across a firm, grassy incline to Pendle's summit.

Descend south from the summit, then veer south-west along a cairned Pendle Way path across the firm slopes of Barley Moor. The path fords a brook, which may be dry in the summer months, and descends along the western edge of Boar Clough. In later stages, the path enters the wider regions of Ogden Clough and joins the outward route by the wooden barrier and Pendle Way signpost. Turn left to return to Barley.

6 Spence Moor

This route from Sabden explores another facet of Pendle, the south side. It climbs from the village made famous by its "treacle mines" to Spence Moor, separated from Pendle Hill by the cavernous, sickle-shaped Ogden Clough. Starting gently in the fields of the Sabden valley it makes for the high ground, discovering Pendle's largest rock outcrop, the Deerstones, before reaching the top of the hill.

Distance:
6 miles/10km

Height gain:
1,050ft/320m

Walking time:
3-4 hours

Start/Finish:
Sabden. GR781376.
There is a small car park
in the village centre and
spaces for a few cars on
the village streets.

Type of walk:
*Farm paths and tracks
and moorland paths. Can
be marshy on the tops
outside the summer
months.*

Be considerate.

From the outer gates of the spired village church, take the lane marked Badger Wells Cottages, which curves right past the charming Cockshotts Farm. Lined by hedgerows of hawthorn, beech, wild rose, and rowan, punctuated by oak trees and tangled with ferns, the lane climbs across high pastureland past New York Farm. There are glimpses through the hedgerow of the emerald Sabden valley to the right and the rounded knoll of Bank Hill to the left. The undulating ridge on the far flanks of the valley has a hill named the Rigg of England, claimed to be the geographical centre of the country.

Ignore the right fork to stay on the Tarmac lane, which now climbs unenclosed towards Ratten Clough Farm. Leave the road just beyond a cattle grid 300yds/m short of the farm for a stony track on the left. Go through a five-bar gate and continue by the fence towards the Churn Clough Reservoir. Turn right by the nearside of the reservoir cottage and follow a well-defined path down to North West Water's perimeter track, which threads between the eastern and northern shores of the lake and some attractive mixed woodland cloaking the lower hill slopes.

Continue west through a five-bar gate from the northwest corner of the reservoir on a clear track across fields. Beyond a step stile by another gate the path runs alongside a rush-filled groove. Double back along a prominent sunken track that climbs northeast away from the pastures to the lower hill slopes. The track degenerates into a narrow footpath which fords an unnamed clough to enter an attractive area dotted with oak and rowan.

In autumn the place is resplendent with colour – the rich vermilion of rowan berries, the yellow-gold, rust and copper of the leaves and bracken, and the dusky green hues of conifer. Looking south, Sabden looks peaceful, tucked in its pastoral valley and shaded by Black Hill.

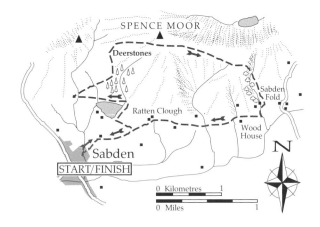

The path continues as a worn, peaty channel running along a crumbling wall at the top edge of the woods encountered earlier. Where the woodland perimeter turns north, the path follows suit and continues in this direction over hillsides cloaked with thick bracken, keeping quite close to a clough on the left. The bracken relents above the 375m contour and the path swings right on a pale grassy spur to the top of the Deerstones.

This is a desolate and windswept place strewn with boulders. Black Hill and the Rigg of England look no more than ripples in the plains of East Lancashire.

The path degenerates beyond Deerstones. Turn north across the grassy top to the ridge wall and follow it east to the ladder stile. Here a well-defined path continues across Spence Moor.

Nelson and Burnley are added to the scene, as are Boulsworth Hill, Black Hameldon and the quarried scars of Hameldon Scout. But the main interest is stirred by Pendle Hill, its dark upper slopes slaked by peat.

The path descends to cross another ladder stile and continues across marshy terrain thickly-clad with rushes and mosses. Occasionally the path tries to trick the walker into the wet stuff, but careful navigation will avoid the worst ground – generally the driest route lies to the left of the rushes.

Leave the path after going through a five-bar gate at GR802390 to descend to the top edge of Cock Clough Plantation. The deep groove of the clough will act as a guide. A gap in the wall by some old ruins marks the start of a path descending east of the woods to Sabden Fold. Go through the farmyard to the left of the house then turn right along the Tarmac lane, which winds through pastureland to assume a westerly direction. Beyond an unnamed stone cottage it becomes an unsurfaced farm track running along the foot of the hillsides. Leave it a few yards beyond a sharp right hand turn (south of Stainscomb) and follow a tree-lined groove west to Ratten Clough Farm. Beyond the farmyard continue along the Tarmac lane used on the outwards route back to Sabden.

7 Earl Crag

Some hills have height on their side, some sheer presence, but others need a helping hand from man to bring them out of the realms of the ordinary. Earl Crag owes much of its popularity to points two and three. It has presence in the form of steep craggy slopes rising from the surrounding farmland. But two large monuments, Lund's Tower and Wainman's Pinnacle, crown its top, luring curious walkers from the valley. This circular walk keeps the company of several delectable streams and becks, and tours a landscape of soft rolling valleys and sombre high Pennine moors.

Distance:
6 miles/10km

Height gain:
770ft/235m

Walking time:
3-4 hours

Start/Finish:
Cowling parish church.
GR968431.

Type of walk:
Moderate. Riverside paths, country lanes and green roads with a steep climb to Earl Crag.

Roadside car parking by church.

Cowling parish has two adjoining villages, as different as chalk and cheese. The main Cowling village consists of terraces and factories strung round the main Colne to Keighley road. It is the birthplace of Lord (Philip) Snowden, the first Labour Chancellor of the Exchequer – there is a nearby monument to him.

Ickornshaw is more rural – a collection of pretty stone cottages sheltered in the little valley of a beck sharing its name, and overlooked by the square-towered parish church.

Follow Cinder Hill Lane, which is signposted from the church as a "Footpath to Wainman's Bottoms". The stony lane climbs gently between the churchyard and the vicarage to high farmland overlooking the little vale of Ickornshaw Brook. Across the brook the view is enlivened by Earl Crag, whose iron-stained gritstone rocks tower above the swelling pastures.

The stony lane ends by a barn and a new grassy track continues beyond a stile and a five-bar gate. It is a delight to walk, being enshrouded by elder, hawthorn, bramble and rowan.

A path joins the route from the right beyond the charming, partially-hidden cottage of Wood House and together they descend to cross the stream on a wooden footbridge. Turn right through a gate into a field and follow the northern banks of the tree-lined stream. Look for a lime kiln in the field to the left.

The path divides at GR980444. The right fork goes by the riverbank; fine after dry spells but otherwise very muddy. The left fork continues by trees at the field's edge. They rejoin by the footbridge at Lane Ends – quite an unusual wooden bridge with stone parapets that must belong to a previous more substantial construction.

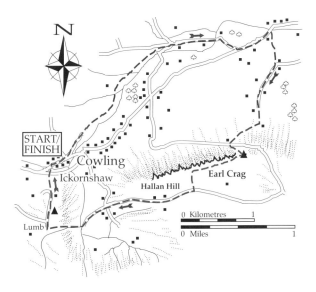

Cross the footbridge and turn left along the country lane, which recrosses the stream and climbs to a T-junction. Turn right here to follow the lane through pleasant rural scenery.

High on the hillside to the left is Stone Gappe Farm, an impressive Georgian mansion surrounded by lush woodland. Charlotte Brontë, who had been employed here as a governess to the children of Mr John Benson Sidgwick, modelled her Gateshead Hall from Jane Eyre *on the house.*

The lane passes the Malsis School, a rather plush boarding school for boys, to meet the Colne Road. Follow the busy road east past the Dog and Gun Inn to Glusburn Bridge – fortunately there is a pleasant tree-lined pavement set well back from the traffic.

Cross the road to go through a gap stile between Bridge Cottage and the bridge over Holme Beck. A little path, confined by a wire fence to the right, follows the stream's southern banks, and divides at the field perimeter. Turn right and head south along the field edge and cross the stile to continue along the concrete drive of Bents Farm (not shown on the South Pennines map). The right of way temporarily abandons the drive on the section between the next gate and the farmhouse. Enter the field on the right on a step stile just beyond the gate and trace the hedge to a gate at the far end of the field – a narrow gap by it allows access back to the track, which climbs south and gently uphill. Beyond a large gate it becomes a pleasing grassy track, lined by thick holly bushes. It climbs past a stone barn and the gradient becomes more severe with views of Earl Crag largely confined to the regions around Lund's Tower – the rest hide behind a tall stone wall on the right.

After passing through the front garden of a picturesque stone-built cottage, climb right, on a concrete drive raking across barren, quarry-scarred slopes beneath Earl Crag's summit fringe. The track meets the road by Brush Farm, a windswept dwelling on the edge of dereliction. Turn left along the road before doubling back to climb the heather and bilberry slopes beneath Lund's Tower.

Sometimes known as Sutton Pinnacle, the dark, castellated folly was constructed by James Lund of Malsis Hall to commemorate the Golden Jubilee of Queen Victoria. It has a spiral staircase to its lofty viewing platform, and what a view it is! Far below the gritstone crags and tumbling moors, the little villages of Cowling and Ickornshaw rest in folds of chequered pastureland, while successive waves of green hills highlighted by wall and hedgerow, rise to Pinhaw Beacon's dark heather cap. To the right the larger mill villages of Sutton and Glusburn guard the gateway to the Aire valley, where Silsden tucks itself between the dusky slopes of Rombald's Moor and Bloomer Hill. Pendle Hill and many of the famous peaks of the Yorkshire Dales stretch out across a pale but busy horizon.

A good track leads along the craggy edge to Wainman's (or Cowling) Pinnacle, a needle-like obelisk built on a huge outcrop of millstone grit.

Historians dispute the origin of this monument. Some say Lady Amcotts had it built in memory of her husband, one of the Wainman family of Carr Head, who was killed at war. Others say it was built in the name of Richard Wainman to mark the Battle of Waterloo or as a memorial to his son who was killed in the Napoleonic War.

Beyond Wainman's Pinnacle and a wall corner the track turns left and heads south past a car park to the lane on Stake Hill. The dark and bare expanses of Ickornshaw Moor dominate all now, wearing a mantle of heather rushes and swaying moor grasses. The lane descends along its fringe, passing stark and rugged sheep farms plucked straight out of a Brontë novel.

When the lane bends right leave it for a track that passes to the right of a small cottage. Beyond a five-bar gate the track becomes a delightful wide green road descending to Dean Brow Beck. A rather dangerous-looking wooden bridge spans the stream; if time does any more damage, it might be better not to use it. Turn right beyond the bridge and climb out on the continuation of the track, which is now overgrown with bracken. It fords Lumb Head Beck and climbs further among chin-high bracken that recedes with height gain. The clough to the left becomes deeper and more confined.

A smattering of trees, including rowans, adds splashes of colour to the scene, especially in September when the red berries are in abundance. Lumb Head Beck plummets down some mossy rocks at the head of the clough, but the scene is unfortunately marred by untidy agricultural surroundings.

Go through the gate at the top of the field and turn right along the farm road, Lumb Lane. The route will now follow the Pennine Way back to Cowling. Lumb Lane bends to the left, but is replaced by a grassy track descending to Lower Summer House. The lane ends and a Pennine Way sign marks the first of two stiles in walls to the right of the austere farmhouse.

Cowling's parish church and Ickornshaw's cottages once again feature in the views ahead as the path descends along the left side of the field to a stile by the main road. The marked footpath immediately opposite has been blocked off with paint daubed on the roadside wall declaring that the Pennine Way path lies to the left. It is, perhaps, a plot by the Black Bull pub to get walkers to sample one of their famous all-day breakfasts – an interesting proposition maybe?

Turn left along the road. The Pennine Way signposted path descends by the Black Bull into Ickornshaw, where a lane threads between the stone cottages to the parish church and the finish of the walk.

8 Clitheroe and Whalley Abbey

As the Ribble nears Clitheroe it slinks into the shadow of Pendle Hill, where tales of intrigue and witchcraft abound. This circular route climbs to the moors at the Nick of Pendle where the whole valley unfurls beneath your feet. It descends to the fields of the Ribble and Calder, where the ruins of Whalley's Cistercian Abbey and Clitheroe's Norman castle feature alongside mysterious Pendle landscapes.

Distance:
11miles/18km

Height gain:
790ft/240m

Walking time:
6 hours

Start/Finish:
Spring Wood Car Park and Picnic Site, Whalley. GR741361.

Type of walk:
A long, but moderately easy circular walk starting with a climb over moorland, then heading across pasture-land on field paths and lanes.

The signposted footpath begins from the roadside 20yds/m south of the car park and skirts the golf course next to Spring Wood. Cross the footbridge at the top end of the wood and follow the faint path heading north-east to a stile at the top left hand corner of the field. After crossing another stile a few yards further, the path turns right, tracing the northern boundary walls of Clerk Hill (a large dwelling). It then passes between two gateposts to a track climbing east to a metalled lane (GR749364).

Turn left along the lane, which degenerates into a track beyond Wiswell Moor Farm. Follow the track on the edge of rough moorland high above Sabden village.

Looking down on the verdant Sabden valley it is difficult to imagine the sinister tales of witchcraft that abound in these parts.

The track emerges at the crest of the high road near the Nick of Pendle. Turn left along the road past the Well Springs pub and the Pendle dry ski run before turning off on a narrow footpath that continues north across rough moorland. It crosses a brook on a small footbridge close to the stone-built Howcroft Barn in the shadow of Pendle Hill's northern slopes.

On a dull day, when the clouds swirl over the dark escarpment's edge, the menacing aura of the Pendle witches begins at last to fill the air. It is a dark tale steeped more in ignorance and superstition than justice. Locals claimed that the two families, led by their elder women, Elizabeth Southern (Old Demdike) from Newchurch and Anne Whittle (Chattox) from Pendle Hall on the banks of the Calder, were black witches.

In 1612, Alizon Device, a granddaughter of Chattox, put a curse on a peddler after he refused to buy some pins. Needless to say, instantly the peddler suffered a stroke and fell to the ground. Alizon admitted her sins to the local magistrate and turned in the Demdike and Chattox clans.

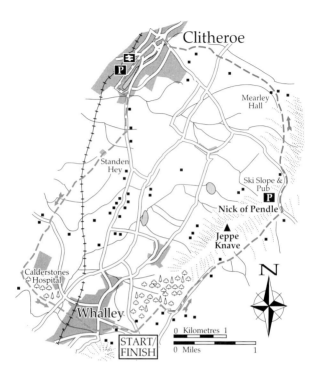

The witches, nineteen in all, were sent for trial at Lancaster and subsequently put to death.

The route continues to the right of another barn and descends along a groove in high pastures through a red gate and on to a farm lane. Turn right along the lane and then left shortly afterwards on a track passing to the right of Mearley Hall. It continues over fields to the A59. Cross the road with care.

A signposted footpath on the other side of the road leads across a narrow metalled lane (the course of the old A59) and traverses more fields. It keeps close to a hedge on the right, which consists of tightly-knit holly, hawthorn and wild roses. The path reaches a farm road leading to the outskirts of Clitheroe. Frequent tourist signs point the way through the pleasant little town to the castle, which perches on a gigantic lime-stone crag at its heart.

The origins of Clitheroe Castle are uncertain, but it is thought to have been constructed around the 12th century for the powerful De Lacey family.

Follow the A671 from the castle south past the Brown Cow pub and out of town. At Barrow Clough Wood (GR739399), a metalled lane, the course of a Roman road, leads south-west to Standen Hey Farm. Go through the right side of the farmyard and continue along the track that crosses the railway line. The path maintains its south-westerly direction across fields that are occasionally used for equestrian events. It passes a stone plinth, part of an ancient cross, en route to Barrow Brook (GR724383).

Providing it is not in spate, ford the brook using the stepping stones (see endnote). After scaling the stile on the opposite banks, continue along a narrow path weaving through woodland to reach the Great Mitton-Whalley road.

Cross the road and follow the stony track tracing the perimeter of Calderstones Hospital. Abandon the track at its southern extremity for a path that heads south-east beyond a small gate, tracing the banks of a streamlet across fields. It passes beneath the road bridge carrying the A59 over the wide, meandering River Calder to join a track that continues under the expansive forty-nine-arched brick railway viaduct. Keep with the track into the village of Whalley via an impressive stone gateway and the ancient ruins of Whalley Abbey.

Abbot Gregory of Norbury and about twenty monks set up the Cistercian Abbey at the turn of the 13th century. Like many other beautiful abbeys, it was destroyed following the Reformation. Its ruins are now open to the public along with a cafe, and the Memory Lane Museum which are also within the grounds. The nearby church is well known for its pre-conquest crosses and is believed to have been built on the site of a church dating back to AD600.

On leaving the abbey, continue along the lane to the main street with its Tudor and Georgian buildings, then turn right towards the river. Just before the bridge follow a ginnel, marked with a public footpath sign, passing some charming cottages on the way to the riverbanks by a large weir. Trace the riverbanks for a short while, until the path diverts past a farm to the B6246 road, which leads back to Spring Wood Car Park.

Alternative route: After prolonged periods of heavy rain, Barrow Brook, north of Calderstones Hospital, floods, making crossing awkward. To avoid this, divert from the main route at Standen Hey Farm to traverse the fields west to Shuttleworth Farm where a left turn along the banks of the River Ribble leads to Mitton Bridge. Follow the road south from here to pick up the main route at GR724381, north of Calderstones.

THE BRONTË MOORS

> *Flowers brighter than the rose bloomed in
> the blackest of heath for her; out of a sullen
> hollow in a livid hillside, her mind could
> make an Eden.*
>
> Charlotte Brontë
> on Emily's love for the Haworth moors.

A little village set on a windy hillside above the Worth valley attracts many thousands of visitors each year, from all over the world. It is all due to three sisters, Anne, Emily and Charlotte Brontë, whose passionate novels brought the dramatic reality of Haworth to astonished Victorian readers.

Such is the impact of these shy, retiring daughters of a village parson that over a century later pilgrims flock to Haworth to see its parsonage, its church and its pretty coffee houses and gift shops. They still trek across its moor to see Emily's waterfalls, Charlotte's seat and the ruins of Heathcliff's house, at Top Withins, and they nearly all go home without seeing the hardship and austerity of the Brontës' 19th-century world.

Search a little wider, as the sisters often did, and the hills get higher, wilder and more dramatic, probably much the same as they would have appeared a century ago.

A vast tract of uninhabited moorland swells to Boulsworth Hill, whose summit, Lad Law, at 1,695ft (517m), is the highest of the Brontë moors. Aping Pendle, which lies across the industrial spread of Burnley and Nelson, it is capped by a rock called the Slaughter Stone, evoking theories of past pagan rituals, of times when man was as relentless as the hills he roamed. Boulsworth gifts walkers with some of the widest panoramas in the South Pennines. The scope is only limited by the atmospheric conditions and the limitations of the human eye.

Boulsworth's last defiant crags overlook the bracken-clad bowl of Widdop, where a remote country lane straddles the hills on its journey from Hebden Bridge to Colne. An even older road, the Gorple Gate track, cuts across the craggy moorland to the west on its way to Worsthorne. It is a fine route used on the climb to dramatic Black Hameldon, whose wet, peaty ridge feeds numerous remote reservoirs.

Many new long distance footpaths have been devised in the region, including the Brontë Way, a 40-mile route from Gawthorpe Hall, Padiham to Oakwell Hall between Bradford and Batley. It links many of the places with Brontë connections both literary and in their real lives.

Much of the heather moorland north of Widdop and west of Haworth is owned by the Savile Estate and is cultivated for shooting. At present there is no right of access to these grouse moors, except on the public footpaths and a handful of permissive routes. Fortunately, Yorkshire Water and North West Water own most of the land in the western regions of Brontë Country and they have created permissive paths and bridleways and have granted good access to the hills.

9 Wycoller and Ickornshaw Moor

This linear route, which is a combination of Pendle Way, Brontë Way and Pennine Way sections, follows the course of Wycoller Beck through the fascinating 17th-century world of Wycoller village before climbing to the wild moors at Watersheddles and Ickornshaw. It is a journey that typifies the wild uplands so cherished by the Brontë sisters and one that offers the walker an insight into the drama that inspired them to write the likes of **Jane Eyre** *and* **Wuthering Heights.**

Distance:
10 miles/16km

Height gain:
950ft/290m

Walking time:
6 hours

Start:
Emmot Arms, Laneshaw Bridge. GR923407.

Finish:
Cowling. GR966428.

Type of walk:
Moderate but long. Farm paths, tracks, and moorland, with some paved ways.

Public Transport:
Bus Nos. 24/25 runs from Burnley/Colne to Keighley stopping at both Laneshaw Bridge and Cowling. Operated jointly by Burnley and Pendle and Keighley & District.

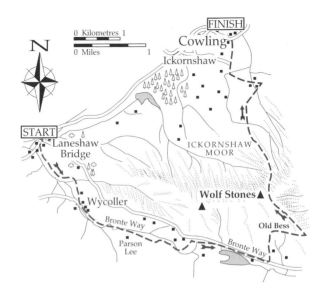

Walk down School Lane (signposted to Haworth), turning right into Carriers Row. Turn left over a stile beyond some cottages and follow a Pendle Way path by Wycoller Beck, crossing a couple of stiles then left by a wall. After going through a gap stile turn right along a track past Lowlands Farm to reach a lane leading into Wycoller, one of the most fascinating villages in the South Pennines. After passing the delightful collection of 17th-century cottages, including a craft shop/cafe, cross the 13th-century twin-arched pack-horse bridge and follow the unsurfaced track past the ancient clapper bridge and the ruins of Wycoller Hall.

In her book, Jane Eyre, *Charlotte Brontë based her Ferndean Manor on the hall, which also features in an 1887 illustrated Haworth edition of the book.*

Beyond the hall the old road passes the information centre, which houses a collection of ancient farm implements and portrays the way of life in the old village. It continues by the beck past Clam Bridge, which is believed to be over 1,000 years old.

Two prominent rocks on the hillside to the left are those of Foster's Leap. The athletic Foster Cunliffe is reputed to have jumped the large gap between the rocks. In another tale a suspected sheep rustler was offered his freedom if he could clear the gap. He did so, on horseback, but being unable to stop on reaching the other side, both horse and rider fell to their deaths.

Beyond Parson Lee the track, often wet outside summer, climbs across high fields to the south of Smithy Clough to meet a lane at the foot of the Boulsworth Hill massif. Turn left along it to traverse the rough grassy moorland of Dove Stones Moor. The grass-covered spoil heaps by the first bend are the remains of limestone excavations and kilns.

Leave the old track as it climbs out of Smithy Clough towards the Haworth road for a waymarked Brontë Way path heading east to the Watersheddles Reservoir. Climb the ladder stile to the road and follow it along the northern shores of the reservoir, which lies in a windswept situation beneath the scabby heather slopes of Crow Hill. To the north the moors are capped by some bold rocks – Wolf Stones. The route will take a closer look later in the day.

After 800yds/m, climb a ladder stile at the entrance to a signposted footpath track, climbing north across Kiln Hill. It turns sharp right across moorland (Bullions) before meeting the Pennine Way. The well-used path climbs by a wall across the grasslands of Old Bess Hill before levelling out on a ridge known as the Sea.

The path reaches heather, and the pathmaker (or breaker) has reached for the stone. Rough-hewn gritstone slabs drape Ickornshaw Moor on a harsh line to the ridge. A wooden stile straddles the fence and the path descends the other side in similar fashion. The odd stretch is unpaved, inviting comparisons with the past.

A number of shooters' chalets line the high pastures at the edge of the moor and the paved path descends to a prominent stone-built one. Here it turns right to become a narrow rush-lined path rigidly following the wall at every turn.

Turn left after crossing a ladder stile and descend, with a wall still to the left, towards the ruins of Higher Dean Hole farm.

A little path to the left of the old ruin descends west to cross a stream, Andrew Gutter, on a wooden foot-bridge. Some steps lead down to another stream, which should be crossed before climbing out to a good grassy track traversing rough pastures to Lumb Hole (GR965420). Here Lumb Head Beck tumbles down rocks into a tree-filled hollow.

The track, now a stony bulldozed one, passes round the head of the clough and above the falls. Continue along the farm road until it bends to the left. Go straight ahead and through a gate here on a grassy track descending to Lower Summer House.

A Pennine Way sign marks the first of two stiles in walls to the right of the austere farmhouse. Cowling's parish church and Ickornshaw's cottages feature in the views ahead as the path descends the left side of the field to a stile at the bottom giving access to the main road and the end of the walk.

10 Withins Height

Literary enthusiasts from all over the world come to Haworth to see the Brontë memorabilia. Anyone who has read the works of the three sisters knows that they were touched by the windswept moors and this Spartan hill village where their father preached. The walk to Top Withins, perhaps the inspiration for Heathcliff's hilltop home, is a classic route through typical South Pennine gritstone landscapes. Here the walker can be transported into the world of Charlotte, Emily and Anne for, with the exception of the signposts, little has changed.

Distance:
6 miles/10km

Height gain:
820ft/250m

Walking time:
4 hours

Start/Finish:
The Penistone Hill Car Park, Haworth.
GR021363.

Type of walk:
A moderate circular walk over rough moorland.

Not recommended in misty conditions.

Follow the car park's drive back to the road at Stanbury Height. A public footpath sign by a patch of wetland, marked on the map as a pool, points the way through a wooden gate and on to the moors.

The narrow path heads west, descending slightly through heather and bilberry past another signpost sited 50yds/m further. Make sure to keep well to the left of the line of grouse-shooting butts near the top of the ridge.

By now the Lower Laithe Reservoir will have come into view to the north beneath Stanbury village, whose gritstone cottages cap a pastured knoll between the Worth valley and the clough of South Dean Beck.

The path gently curves to the right to join a stony farm track on the lip of the South Dean Beck. The track, a part of the Brontë Way, bends south-west and narrows to become no more than a footpath over the moors. It is now surrounded by reeds, bracken, heather and a few foxgloves.

A few farms, some sadly in ruins, punctuate the scene to the right but a distant line of gritstone crags lends some excitement in the narrowing clough.

On approaching the crags, the path descends by a series of steps into the now rugged clough. A stone footbridge, grandly named the Brontë Bridge, spans the beck.

A plaque informs that the original bridge was washed away by flash floods in May 1989 and that this one was rebuilt in 1990. A signpost also informs in English and Oriental ideograms that the Brontë waterfalls are to the left; in fact you can see them by turning your head to the left. In summer they are little more than a trickle over mossy

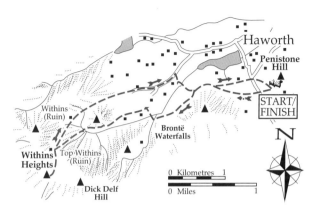

slabs but, after periods of high rainfall, they are much more impressive and it is not hard to see why the Brontë sisters loved them so much. A little footpath climbs a heathery spur to the left for those who want to inspect them more closely. The nearby Brontë Chair is a rock where Charlotte would occasionally sit to write poetry.

Cross the little bridge and follow the Brontë Way up the bouldered slopes. Go through a kissing gate to the northern rim of the clough near a ruined farm. Leave the Brontë Way and turn left to follow the well-defined path south-west parallel to the clough, ignoring the ladder stile at the top of the field and to the right. Top Withins can now be seen in views ahead, high on the moor, next to a big tree.

The path fords South Dean Beck (at GR986356) and climbs to a flagged track just short of Top Withins. The old ruin gets rather less inviting with each passing year; it has now lost its roof and visitors are told to keep out for safety reasons. A plaque states, "This farmhouse has been associated with Wuthering Heights, the Earnshaw home in Emily

Brontë's novel. The building, even when complete, bore no resemblance to the house she described but the situation may have been in her mind when she wrote of the moorland setting of the Heights."

To get the best out of the walk, continue along the flagged path to the top of the moor – to see the view on the other side. The path arrives halfway between Round Hill and Dick Delf Hill.

Black Hameldon and the Walshaw and Gorple Reservoirs dominate the scene. On the southern horizon are Stoodley Pike (look out for its monument) and Blackstone Edge; to the north the wild rangy flanks of Boulsworth Hill dominate all.

Unfortunately there is no right of way along the ridge, otherwise the route could have descended by way of Oxenhope Stoop Hill. So, return to Withins Height and continue on the flagged Pennine Way track past the whitewashed Upper Heights Farm (camping) and the pretty stone-built Lower Heights Farm (lovely gardens). Ignore Pennine Way and Brontë Way signs which divert to the left and right, respectively.

Keep on the track known as Back Lane until GR003367 opposite a farmhouse (left). A stile in the stone wall to the right marks the start of a field path, which descends steeply to cross South Dean Beck by a wooden footbridge. The path goes right of some trees then swings left to a cross a stile. It then climbs out of the clough to a ladder stile giving access to the stony Brontë Way track encountered early in the day.

Follow the track to the road above the Lower Laithe Reservoir then climb on the signposted route across Stanbury Height to the car park.

11 Boulsworth Hill

Boulsworth Hill's wide expanses of heather and weird-shaped crags make it one of the most popular tops in the South Pennines. At 1,695ft/517m, it is the highest peak in a vast tract of moorland stretching from the Calder valley at Todmorden to the Aire valley at Keighley. Much of the hill is out of bounds to walkers, but two routes can be combined for a splendid walk from the northern side. This walk chooses an interesting approach from Wycoller, and tackles the steep northern flanks of the hill, but rewards its conquerors with a breathtaking view across the industrial towns of East Lancashire to the hills and mountains of Bowland, Pendle and the Yorkshire Dales.

Distance:
8 miles/13km

Height gain:
1,115ft/340m

Walking time:
5 hours

Start/Finish:
Car park on the
Trawden-Wycoller lane.
GR926395.

Type of walk:
A moderate circular walk on farm lanes, with a stiff climb over rough, wet moorland.

The lane from the car park dips into Wycoller village and transports the visitor into the 17th century, with picturesque weavers' cottages huddled into a narrow verdant vale.

Wycoller once thrived on the exploits of both farming and weaving. On the decline of those industries it was purchased by the water authorities who had intended to construct a reservoir here, but never did. In 1973, Lancashire County Council bought much of the area and turned it into the delightful country park it is today.

Wycoller Hall, now in ruins, was built in the 16th century as a country house for the wealthy Cunliffe family. The last squire, spendthrift Henry Cunliffe, built up debts. On his death in 1774, the estate was divided and sold to repay them and the hall was left to decay. It would have been empty in the time of Charlotte Brontë, but the location inspired Fearndean Manor in her book, Jane Eyre.

Cross the playful Wycoller Beck on the fine twin-arched packhorse bridge, which has origins in the 13th century.

There are two more unusual bridges on the route through the village. The Clapper Bridge, opposite the ruins of Wycoller Hall, consists of three slabs of stone spanning two piers. Continue along the lane to see the more austere Clam Bridge, reputed to be more than 1,000 years old and formed by a single slab of gritstone. It has had a hard time of late, being swept off its perch during flash floods in 1989 and 1991.

The metalled lane follows the banks of Wycoller Beck and continues south-east through the tree-lined dene. There are fish, including brown trout in the beck – a fact that the herons and kingfishers know only too well.

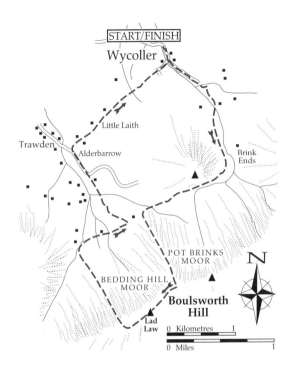

Wycoller

Little Laith

Trawden

Alderbarrow

Brink
Ends

POT BRINKS
MOOR

BEDDING HILL
MOOR

Boulsworth
Hill

N

Lad
Law

0 Kilometres 1

0 Miles 1

Abandon the lane for a track across the beck towards
Dean House Farm. A number of paths meet hereabouts (many not marked on pre-1995 Outdoor
Leisure Maps). This route, signposted initially to
Trawden, begins from a stile and thence south-east
across a small field to cross Turnhole Clough, a tribu-
tary of Wycoller Beck, via a wooden footbridge
(GR937388). A path then turns left along the upper
banks of the splendid wooded glen before entering
the woodland for a brief spell. It continues across
wild, bracken-clad fellsides scattered with crag and

boulder. Boulsworth Hill's northern slopes in the view ahead whet the appetite.

The path descends to the banks of the stream before climbing to join the bridleway from Brink End. The old packhorse route soon veers south-west and becomes intermittently paved with weather-beaten slabs of millstone grit that appear to be sinking into the rushy moors. To the right are high, declining pastures. To the left, beyond the groove of Saucer Hill Clough, the rough pallid course grasses rise to the serrated profiles of the Great Chaucer Stones.

The ascent of Boulsworth Hill, a North West Water courtesy route, begins by the lonely farm of Spoutley Lumb on a concrete road that climbs south-east to a small reservoir. From here, a waymarked path rises steeply on the concave peaty slopes of Pot Brinks Moor. A few small gritstone outcrops (The Little Chair Stones) come into view on gaining the ridge.

The ensuing route across the wide peaty ridge climbs easily to the Weather Stones, an impressive group of weirdly eroded crags whose nooks and crannies offer good shelter against the elements. They are, perhaps, a good lunch spot.

Boulsworth Hill's summit, Lad Law, lies a little to the west, marked by a concrete trig point set close to gritstone crags. Some say the place has a sinister past. The very name has its origins in the Celtic word "Llad", meaning slaughter, and "Law" meaning hill, suggesting that here was a Druid altar of sacrifice. More pragmatic historians believe that the rock is no more than an old boundary stone, eroded by time and the harsh elements.

Whatever its past, the summit gives striking views over the industrial towns of Colne, Nelson and Burnley to the whaleback of Pendle Hill and, further afield, to Bowland, Pen y Ghent, Ingleborough and the Lakeland fells.

The descent begins on a well-defined path across Bedding Hill Moor. It returns to the track used earlier, only a little further to the west. This time turn right and follow the track back to Spoutley Lumb Farm. Climb the ladder stile at the far end of the farm and follow the line of the wall on the left. At its termination continue in the same direction through a grassy hollow to reach a concrete bridge over a stream.

A short detour to the left leads to Lumb Spout, a pleasant waterfall cascading over a sandstone cliff in a sylvan hollow of oak, ash and rowan. The falls are almost certainly man-made for the course of the river has clearly been diverted to the top of the cliffs.

Return to the bridge, where the route continues across fields, passing to the right of a farm (Lodge Moss) before meeting a narrow country lane. Follow this downhill to a large mill at Hollin Hall, south of Trawden.

Take the track (signposted "To Wycoller and Raven's Rock") at the far end of the mill. It climbs across pastures and turns sharp left towards Far Wanless Farm. Leave it here and cross the dilapidated stile for a path bearing half right (east) by a wall. After passing Little Laithe Farm the route continues north-east by the wall, passing to the left of Germany Farm and Raven's Rock Farm, crossing several primitive stiles and a couple of dykes en route. Beyond Raven's Rock Farm the path descends through a young plantation of larch, birch, rowan and alder before meeting a stony farm track, which leads back into Wycoller village – a cup of tea and a scone at the cafe perhaps, before heading back up the lane to the car park?

12 Heasandford to Thursden

This linear walk follows the Brontë Way route through the attractive, sylvan valleys of Swinden Water and Thursden Brook. It is an ideal saunter when time is short, especially in the spring or autumn when the woods are alive with colour.

Distance:
4 1/4 miles/7km

Height gain:
625ft/190m

Walking time:
3 hours

Start:
Heasandford.
Netherwood Road Car Park. GR858335.

Type of walk:
An easy walk on woodland and field paths.

A car would be required at both ends of the walk.

Finish:
Thursden Car Park/ Picnic Site, 2 miles/3km east of Widdop Reservoir. GR902352.

Beyond the car park Netherwood Road becomes an unsurfaced track. Follow it east across the bridge over the River Don close to the confluence with the River Brun. The track soon divides. Take the right fork, then follow the footpath to the right, which is highlighted by Burnley Way (yellow and black) and the Brontë Way (raspberry and yellow) waymarks.

The narrow path winds through young mixed woodland on the northern side of the Swinden valley. Ignore the footbridge over Swinden Water and continue through thickets of birch, oak, bramble, wild rose and holly. The path temporarily leaves the cover of woodland at a stile to cross a field but the scattered trees of Houghton Hag thicken and the path resumes in the splendid setting of a crag strewn wooded valley.

Houghton Hag is a fine example of ancient broadleaved woodland managed under the coppice system, in which the timber is harvested regularly, allowing sunlight to penetrate the canopy and encouraging the wide range of wild flowers that grow today.

After tracing a quarry track at the far edge of Houghton Hag, the way reaches the grass-covered dam of Lee Green Reservoir. The Burnley Way has diverted to the left for Extwistle Hall and will not rejoin the route until Park Woods in the Thursden valley.

Lee Green is one of three reservoirs in the Swinden valley built by 1864 to supply the needs of Burnley's industries.

Climb the steps in the wall and continue across the dam's causeway, then turn left on a walled track along the southern shores of the lake.

The track, lined by bramble and rosebay willowherb, terminates at the road, but the Brontë Way continues on the Tarmac farm lane immediately opposite. It swings left through pastureland and beneath the dams of the Swinden Reservoirs. Once past Ing Hey Farm and its outbuildings keep to the lower track, which arcs round the spur of Twist Hill. On entering the pastoral Holden Clough it becomes a sunken

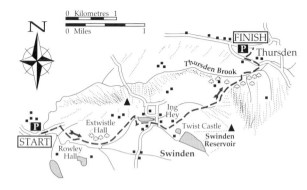

grassy track descending to cross the stream before climbing to Sweet Well House. Some steps in the stone wall to the left give access to the farm's Tarmac drive, which climbs to the Pike Low ridge.

The airy ridge gives wide views across East Lancashire to the sea and includes Burnley and Blackburn, framed by the hills of Bowland, Pendle and Hameldon. It is a striking sight close to sunset.

Leave the lane as it bends to the left and climb the ladder stile over the wall. The path underfoot across the field is non-existent, but be content to follow the direction of the Brontë Way arrow north to a group of stony mounds.

The Thursden Scars, as the mounds are known, are the remains of limestone hushings, where dams were constructed and watercourses diverted to wash out the boulders. Limestone was an important mineral in the 17th and 18th centuries, needed for tanning, enriching acid soils, and the manufacture of mortar and whitewash. From the hushings the walker looks down on the Thursden valley, a deep hollow where fields and woods meet the high moors of Widdop and Boulsworth Hill.

A prominent track descends east into the Thursden valley. It gives up the ghost by a dilapidated wall and the path turns left downhill towards the brook. Turn right using a step stile to straddle the wall on the right, then descend further through Park Wood to cross the brook on a wooden footbridge. The well-defined path turns right along the northern banks of the brook to reach a country lane.

Turn left along the winding lane, which is thickly lined with bramble and roses. Wine and jam-makers would find a trip here most fruitful.

After climbing past two farmhouses leave the lane and turn right on a signposted footpath (GR899349) raking across a steep grassy bank to a stile at the back of the Thursden Car Park.

13 Gorple and Widdop

At Widdop and Gorple the underlying gritstone breaks free from its tussocky moorland crust to dress the tops and valleysides with a dusky hat. Here the South Pennines are at their widest and arguably their wildest. This circular walk follows an ancient packhorse trail to the craggy bowl of Widdop and returns across Extwistle Moor, whose slopes are a little greener, a little less remote, and a pleasing contrast. On this route the walker feels a sense of walking not just through the hills, but also the barriers of time and history.

Distance:
8 miles/13km

Height gain:
1,050ft/320m

Walking time:
5 hours

Start/Finish:
The village green,
Worsthorne.
GR876324.

Type of walk:
A high moorland walk
above the industrial
conurbations of East
Lancashire.

Gorple Road is an ancient packhorse route connecting Worsthorne and Heptonstall, that would have been used for the transport of lime and cloth.

From Worsthorne's village green, pass to the north of the Victorian spired church and along the signposted Gorple Road, which soon becomes an unsurfaced track climbing straight-as-a-die east past farms and allotments. Hurstwood Reservoir comes into view in a hollow to the right, surrounded by conifers on three sides and the grassy spoil heaps of a disused limestone quarry on the fourth.

The southern slopes of Wasnop Edge rear up to the left as the old road enters the high combe of Hurstwood Brook. Finally, the pastures are left behind at a five-bar gate and a spacious moorland scene takes over with Hameldon (L) and Black Hameldon (R) capturing the horizon.

After fording Hurstwood Brook the track meanders round the high hill slopes of Hameldon. Some prominent rocks, the Hare Stones, jut out from the middle of the pass ahead. The Gorple Road, however, keeps to the northern side, passing beneath the Gorple Stones, where a vast tract of steep, boulder-strewn hillside is crested with crag.

New views open up on reaching the pass. Gorple Upper Reservoir, an isolated sheet of water surrounded by ancient pastures long returned to the moor is shaded by Black Hameldon's steep northern end and framed by some shapely outcrops on Shuttleworth Moor. It is one of two reservoirs built between 1927 and 1934 to serve Halifax. Looking back, another reservoir, Cant Clough, occupies a hollow and leads the eye to Thieveley Scout, a line of gritstone cliffs fringing Cliviger Gorge.

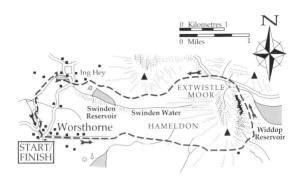

The track has changed its name: it is now the Gorple Gate Track. It continues east, high above the reservoir and the derelict pastures to the bold gritstone crags of Gorple Gate, which run down the spine of Shuttleworth Moor. Beyond the Gate, the track descends north-east with the expansive Widdop Reservoir appearing in its deep crag-ringed basin. The path swings north to enter the basin beneath Clough Head Stones. Take the left branch at a junction of tracks above the reservoir and continue north across wet rushy ground. Looking back the weird rocks of Cludders Slack fringe the slopes above a small coniferous plantation.

The Widdop Reservoir holds 633 million gallons of water and was completed in 1878 to supply Halifax. The engineer, Edward La Trobe Bateman, who had attended the opening of the Suez Canal the previous year, was influenced by Egyptian design and this manifests itself in the valve house at the southern end of the dam.

The path crosses Widdop's feeder stream on a little

footbridge and climbs out to the Colne to Hebden Bridge lane, which hereabouts is a narrow strip of Tarmac undulating over high, bracken-clad moorland. Turn left along the lane and climb on it to the top of the pass.

Follow the signposted footpath west across Extwistle Moor. Never in doubt, the grooved track descends into the hollow of Swinden Water, passing beneath an area of old coal pits and quarries under Delph Hill. The Swinden Reservoirs come into view in an area which, in contrast to Gorple, seems very green. On Twist Hill the path, now fainter, traverses verdant sheep pastures with gates in the crosswalls.

The path joins the Burnley Way long distance route on an unsurfaced lane that rounds the smaller reservoir before meeting the road at Swinden Bridge. Cross the road and follow the track along the south side of Lee Green Reservoir, turning right along its dam. After climbing a step stile in the wall at the base of the dam, turn left on a path running parallel with Swinden Water, the outflow stream. The path crosses several stiles as it ambles through the pleasant valley, staying close to the stream to enter a narrow strip of woodland.

Leave the Burnley Way at a wooden stile to the left of the path and descend to cross the river using some stepping stones. Climb the far banks to a marker post with yellow arrows that show the way across a field towards Wood Hey Farm, to the left.

Turn right after crossing a stile and head south on the farm track, then left at the junction with the unmade road from Higher Cote. It passes the recreation ground and by a mill into Brownside Road, which leads back to Worsthorne's village green.

14 Black Hameldon

Black Hameldon lies at the heart of the lofty expanse of moorland rising from the green fields and factory chimneys of East Lancashire. Its summit, known as Hoof Stones Height, crowns a broad, marshy ridge not 5 miles/8km from the centre of Burnley. The very name, Black Hameldon, which means black scarred hill, invokes images of a dark satanic place. Indeed, on a sunless day, when its peaty upper slopes are at their blackest, the reputation would appear deserved. This route is one of the finest walks in the South Pennines, guiding the walker into some of the widest, wildest landscapes in the region.

Distance:
9¼ miles/15km

Height gain:
1,330ft/405m

Walking time:
5 hours

Start/Finish:
Roadside car park,
2 miles/3km east of
Widdop Reservoir.
GR958324.

Type of walk:
Moderate to hard walk on peaty moorland paths and tracks.

Public Transport:
H2 Blake Dean bus from Hebden Bridge on Sundays from Easter to the end of October.

A stile on the lower of two hairpin bends above the road bridge gives access to Blake Dean where a delightful but faint path traces the upper fringes along the gritstone rocks of Ridge Scout.

Graining Water rushes playfully through the tight, bracken-clad valley whose head is spanned by the grassy inclines of the Gorple Lower Reservoir's dam.

A paved packhorse route, the course of the Pennine Way, comes up to meet the route. Double-back along it and descend to cross two wooden footbridges over Graining Water and the outflow of the reservoir. The path, still paved, climbs out of the valley to the reservoir keeper's house at Gorple Cottages.

It might seem strange when passing the place in the light of a summer's day, but this was the scene of a tragedy when the reservoir keeper was caught out in a blizzard, dying on the moors he knew so well.

Follow Yorkshire Water's track over the dam and along the northern shores of the lake, passing some small weather-beaten spruce plantations that cling to the pallid moorland slopes. The track ends by the dam of the Gorple Upper Reservoir. Here a well-used path climbs north past the shapely gritstone tors of Shuttleworth Moor to the Gorple Gate track, which has climbed from the Widdop Reservoir.

For those who have never seen Widdop, it is worth a diversion east to see the lake basking in a crag-fringed bowl of bracken and moor grass.

Otherwise, turn left for the Gorple Stones. If the day is a dull one, Black Hameldon will be true to its name, for its peaty northern end reflects a stark and sullen aura over the dilapidated pastures and upper lake.

The Gorple Stones are an impressive collection of huge gritstone boulders capped with crag. It would be worth the effort to detour to their rim to get a superior view of the surrounding moors.

Abandon the track on reaching its apex beneath the Stones. An extremely smelly bit of marsh near the start of the new south-westerly path needs intelligent circumnavigation to reach terra firma at the Hare Stones.

Crowning a moorland col at the foot of Black Hameldon's northern end, the Hare Stones are well placed for a refreshment stop; their nooks and crannies always provide good shelter from the prevailing wind. (Hoof Stones Height, the main summit, has no shelter.) Views are good too, with the tiered crags of Thieveley Scout rising from Cliviger Gorge beyond Cant Clough Reservoir, which languishes amid the declining peaty slopes of Worsthorne Moor.

The path climbs on Black Hameldon's peat-scarred slopes to gain the broad, marshy ridge, which spans just over a mile (1,700m) to the summit at Hoof Stones Height. Here some shallow pools, that can be dry in summer, surround a concrete trig point.

Unfortunately, the broadness of the ridge restricts views of the Calder valley, but the airy situation provides wide panoramas of the hills of the Peak District and the Yorkshire Dales. It is also a grand place to view the whaleback escarpment of Pendle Hill, rising from the chimneys of Padiham, and Burnley.

The way down from Hoof Stones Height is by a new permissive route marked only on the post-1995 Outdoor Leisure Maps. A path on the ground has already developed and descends east on peaty slopes, marked by waymarking posts to the ruins of an old reservoir dam.

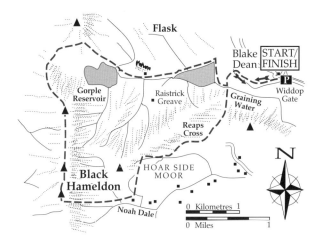

This lies at the head of Noah Dale in the upper reaches of Colden Water. Hereabouts dilapidated stone walls frame ruinous farmsteads – a testament to the tough times that forced country folk out of their homes, some to the cities, some to the New World. It is all very different from the valley just four miles downstream, where thick woodland cloaks the steep sides.

The best route back to Widdop follows a narrow path north, still guided by the posts, climbing Hoarside Moor. Dwarfed and isolated scrub birch trees are sparsely scattered across this barren, tussocky wasteland. They make a strange addition to the scene. Leave the path just beyond the crossing of Fleight Clough for an indistinct narrow track across the southern flanks of Raistrick Greave Hill.

The area is deserted by humankind and birdwatchers will be in their element. Mallard, teal, grouse, moorhen, lapwing, skylark and curlew may be joined by whooper swans, buzzard and raven.

On reaching a wall corner (at GR938302), the path becomes more obvious and follows the wall to Reaps Cross, which lies in pieces. Surely this is worthy of renovation?

The view north has now opened up to reveal sleek-profiled hills that stretch from the reservoirs of Gorple and across the horizon – pale and grassy around Hameldon in the west, etched with dark heather over the Haworth Moors to the east. They are embellished by some shapely crags and outcrops, the most prominent ones being the Gorple Stones, those fringing the Widdop Reservoir (the lake is hidden from here) and the rocky diadem on Lad Law.

The path continues east from the cross for 300yds/m to a stony cart track linking Colden and Widdop. Follow the old packhorse route north down to the reservoir keeper's cottage beneath the grass-cloaked dam of the Gorple Lower Reservoir. Retrace earlier steps down into the little valley of Graining Water, across the bridges and back to the car park along the upper edge of Blake Dean.

15 Hebden Bridge to Haworth

This splendid walk links two fine Pennine towns, and takes a look at Heptonstall's quaint cobbled streets, weavers' cottages, and two churches before descending into Crimsworth Dean. The old Haworth road climbs to the Pennine rooftop before plunging into the Worth valley and Brontë Country. Being a linear walk it requires the use of two cars – one parked at either end, or the use of public transport (see below).

Distance:
8 miles/13km

Height gain:
1,670ft/510m

Walking time:
4-5 hours

Start:
Car park Hebden Bridge. GR993273.

Finish:
Haworth. GR030373.

Type of walk:
A walk on ancient roads and tracks traversing both woodland and farm pasture before straddling the high Pennine moors.

Public Transport:
No. 500 Bus (Keighley DT) from Haworth to Hebden Bridge. Four per day summer weekdays (none Sundays): Wednesday and Saturday, only in winter.

Take the Todmorden road out of Hebden Bridge past the antique shops, the book shops and cafes to Stoney

Lane. Climb a long flight of gritstone steps, which squeeze between buildings to the Slack road. Turn right on the road, then double back on a path (signposted "To Hell Hole Rocks"). This climbs steadily through trees emerging on the hillsides high above Colden Clough.

There are good views of Calderdale, whose roads, railways and canals thread through a twisting valley filled with trees and with scattered mills and dusky gritstone-built cottages.

As height is gained, Stoodley Pike and its monument rise above Erringden Moor.

Ignore paths to the right, keeping to the edge all the way to the huge (Hell Hole) rocks. A flight of steps to their far left rakes up the hillsides towards Heptonstall. At the top, by some new and ill-sited housing, a path leads into the village past two churches.

The older church, dedicated to St. Thomas à Beckett, is an interesting shell, built in the 13th century but later enlarged. The newer church was built after St. Thomas' was destroyed in a storm in 1847.

Heptonstall is one of the finest hill villages in Yorkshire, a good example of an old weaving village before the power loom took over and the population moved downhill to the modern settlements of Hebden Bridge and Todmorden. Its narrow cobbled streets are fascinating and one could spend much more time here – but Haworth beckons.

Turn left up the cobbled main street past the two inns and right along Townfield Lane. Beyond the cottages it becomes a walled track across high meadows with the tree-filled depression of Hebden Dale ahead. Turn half left across fields when the lane ends on the approach to Lea Bank, to reach the lane to Slack. The

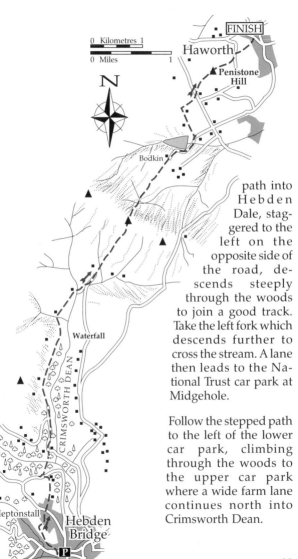

path into Hebden Dale, staggered to the left on the opposite side of the road, descends steeply through the woods to join a good track. Take the left fork which descends further to cross the stream. A lane then leads to the National Trust car park at Midgehole.

Follow the stepped path to the left of the lower car park, climbing through the woods to the upper car park where a wide farm lane continues north into Crimsworth Dean.

On the opposite side of the dean, crowning slopes of pasture and attractive woodland, is a dark gritstone obelisk, the Pecket War Memorial, not unlike a miniature Stoodley Pike monument.

Many will want to make a detour from the lane to see Abel Cross. To do so, go through the stile in the wall to the left a short way beyond the last pine trees of Crimsworth woods. The old Celtic cross lies south-west across the field by a farm track.

Return to the main track and continue north. Beyond Nook Farm (ruins) it is a worthwhile detour to see Lumb Hole waterfalls, which cascade in a woodland setting by an old packhorse bridge. Otherwise continue through the dean, descending rough pastures to cross Paddock Beck, an offspring of Crimsworth Beck, to meet the old Haworth Road at Grain Water Bridge.

Turn left up the narrow Tarmac lane, which climbs steeply past Lane Head Farm where it degenerates into a walled stony track straining up bleak pastures. Beyond Stairs Dyke, the last farmhouse, the pastures are replaced by moorland. The little road sneaks over slopes with intriguing names like Stairs Swamp to the ridge at Top of Stairs.

Looking back, Crimsworth Dean channels the vision towards Stoodley Pike. The transition from bleak to beautiful, from desolate to thriving, is there for all to see. Just peeping over the slopes of Wadsworth Moor are the dusky tops of Boulsworth Hill and Black Hameldon. Strange contraptions cap Oxenhope Moor to the east – they are part of the Bradford University's Laboratory. At the time of writing, they are studying the apparent brightness of the stars, global warming and other meteorological statistics.

The path, now a grassy one, continues over the wind-swept top in glorious style.

The views of distant eastern hills include the craggy, heather-clad Barden Moor, above Skipton and Wolf Stones, above the Worth valley. Towns and villages, such as Keighley, with its high rise flats, and Haworth, are scattered among the hills.

As it descends, the track finds a reed-lined grassy channel through old quarries, and crosses a water company leat.

The Leeshaw Reservoir basks in its hollow below, breaking up the web of emerald fields and dark walls. To the right, the alien white windmills of Ovenden Moor trap the breeze into creating surplus electricity for the valleys.

The track has become a walled stony lane again, but its verges are thick with heather and bilberry. Further down it is embellished with colourful rosebay willowherb and vetch. Little Oxenhope becomes increasingly prominent in views ahead, tucked comfortably between folds in the hills.

Beyond Bodkin Farm the track meets a Tarmac lane running along the bottom edge of the dam. Looking downstream there is a little mill with its chimney still intact. Turn left along the pale gravelly track to the left of a stand of trees and climb north-west to Westfield Farm. Beyond the farm maintain direction and go through a primitive plywood gate. The track is now an overgrown rutted one, tracing a wall to the right. At the top of the second field turn right to climb the stile next to a waymarking post. An unmade lane continues east past Drop Farm (cafe and B&B) to Moorside Lane opposite the public conveniences.

Turn left along the lane, then right a few strides later,

to follow a pale gravel track across Penistone Hill. There is an abundance of tracks and car parks here, but the roads are well signposted. Take the left fork, which heads for the northern edge of the moor.

Beyond the last car park (GR020365) the gravel ends, to be replaced by a grassy path ("To Haworth") past some picnic tables. To the left side there is more willowherb, to the right, quarry boulders and heather.

Once across the road at the far side of Penistone Hill, continue along the path to Haworth Church, a neat stony track passing a couple of cottages. At its end turn left along a paved path past a goat pen and aviary. It emerges in Haworth's village centre after passing in front of the parish church, where many of the Brontës were buried.

Haworth usually buzzes with tourists who clamber up and down the steep cobbled main street. The inns, cafes, gift shops and galleries will have a less austere facade than the main street of Brontë times, but otherwise little has changed.

16 Oxenhope Moor

This circular visits the edges of Brontë Country from the little mill village of Oxenhope. It climbs across Oxenhope Moor to its summit at Nab Hill. Save it for a clear day or evening, when the views will be pleasant and far-reaching.

Distance:
4 1/4 miles/7km

Height gain:
785ft/240m

Walking time:
2-3 hours

Start/Finish:
Jew Lane, Oxenhope, east of the Post Office.

Type of walk:
Field paths, rough moorland and quarry tracks.

Oxenhope, which means remote valley of the ox, is an attractive stone-built village made famous by being the terminus of the Keighley and Worth Valley Railway. The line, built by the Midland Railway in 1867 to service the many woollen mills that once prospered, closed in 1961, but was rescued by enthusiasts who have run it as a steam railway ever since. The line has been immortalised on celluloid on many occasions, the most famous being, **The Railway Children.** *Nearby Bents Farm was the Three Chimneys of that film.*

Climb between the converted mill and the overgrown cemetery on Jew Lane, then take the right fork, marked with a cul-de-sac signpost and Brontë Way marker (raspberry and yellow). The lane descends past stone-built cottages and degenerates into a grassy track. After climbing to the right of a house, turn left on an enclosed path to the dam of Leeming Reservoir. Further Brontë Way signs point the way on a stony farm lane heading south-east across fields above the reservoir.

Leave the lane as it veers right for Lower Isle Farm and follow a faint waymarked path across fields. Several stiles are strategically placed in cross walls. The path descends to cross a stream, Nan Scar, and circumvent the pool by the head of the reservoir. It climbs along the edge of some woodland. A helpful Brontë Way sign (BW) shows the path wiggling left to cross a little slabbed bridge over Stony Hill Clough, then immediately right to climb fields above its east banks.

Keep following the Brontë Way through a gap stile in one crosswall and over a ladder stile, which gives access to a bridge over a water company leat. The moor ahead beckons as the farm pastures are left behind. The path follows the line of a sunken rushy track. Marker posts show the way round two left dog-legs in the route. A three-way footpath signpost marks the leaving of the Brontë Way. This route follows the public path along Hambleton Lane, a wide, rutted grassy track climbing south across Thornton Moor. Ignore the much greener path by the reservoir leat.

Thornton Moor Reservoir, a wild and woolly sheet of water, comes into view as the old packhorse road gains height. Leave the track through a five-bar gate on the right (GR047332), and climb along a sunken grassy

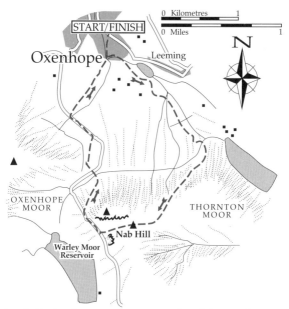

track that rakes south-west to the old quarries on Hambleton Top.

The quarries were once worked by over 300 men, who toiled to provide the much-needed stone for the building of mills, houses and reservoirs.

For some time, the wind turbines on Ovenden Moor have been peeping from behind the quarry-scarred, serrated summits of Nab Hill and Hambleton Top, but now they are in full view. Mill-studded farmland capped by the darker moors spreads across the northern skyline in a view across Oxenhope and down the Worth valley. Oakworth squats on a distant hillside, while Haworth stays hidden behind the lower slopes of Penistone.

A narrow track roughly traces the edge to the most prominent cairn/shelter on Nab Hill. From here it leads to a deeply sunken quarry track which heads south-west to the high moorland road overlooking the Warley Moor Reservoir, a huge and desolate lake that is home to a sailing club.

Turn right along the road, then leave it for a signposted path on the right. The new path is faint at first, but an old rushy track soon takes over to pass the top end of rough walled pastures. At the end of the third, turn left across the dilapidated top wall and follow the wall downhill to a stile, then cross a leat by a little bridge to meet the road again. A signpost opposite points the way across more rough fields. An arrow highlights a change of direction across horribly tussocky ground (no path). Fortunately, a few strides to the left a raised grassy embankment avoids the worst ground and conveys the route to the roadside stile at GR033334.

Turn left along the lane for 400yds/m to the second of two closely-spaced footpath signposts. An intermittent path traces the edge of a deepening ravine east of Hill House Edge and overlooking Oxenhope. Rowan trees and bracken add splashes of colour – a splendid sight at autumn time. Shortly after going through a little gate in a wall, the path turns right though a walled alleyway over a bracken-tangled leat, then left to descend further into the ravine. It passes to the left of an old wall and through an area of wild rose bushes and hawthorns. Keep to the right of a wall corner to pass to the right of a stone farmhouse on the edge of dereliction. Go through the stile in the wall ahead and descend the field by a couple of mill ponds. On reaching the substantial Wadsworth House, turn left along the lane, which climbs past some cottages to rejoin Jew Lane to conclude the walk.

THE CLOTH CAP HILLS

This diverse group owes more to the practicalities of book layout than a relationship to each other for there are two distinct ranges. One climbs from the back streets of Burnley, spanning 12 miles/19km across Thieveley Pike to Shore Moor above Rochdale: the other is a moorland horseshoe rising to Scout Moor and Cowpe Moss above Rawtenstall.

The region is drained by the Irwell, the Roche, the Spodden and their tributaries. They turn out to be industrial rivers but, as the hills themselves are working class, it does not seem to matter.

In past centuries the hills have been subjected to the ravages of mining, quarrying, reservoir building and face further incursions from wind turbines.

If this all sounds gloomy, these cloth cap hills have merits: in the main they are less boggy than the Brontë Moors and those of Calderdale and, in the central regions, they are far more wild and remote. Maybe these lofty hills are not so rural as some, maybe the little cottages are not so quaint, but the prospect of picking out town and city landmarks does add appeal to the day.

Thieveley Pike, the most northerly of the hills, is more like the Calderdale hills in character, showing a bold facade of tiered crag to the Cliviger Gorge. Next to it, the sleek grassy escarpment of Inchfield Moor is considered to be Todmorden's highest hill, but one with its roots firmly to the west in Rossendale.

The hills to the south across the hollow of Ramsden Clough include Rough Hill, Hades Hill and Shore Moor. These scarred grassy domes offer some of the most remote walking in the South Pennines. Mainly trackless they provide a stiff test of navigation, even on a clear day.

Long distance walkers could tackle the Rossendale Way, a 45-mile circular round the edges of the borough (see Long Distance Routes for details).

17 Thieveley Pike and Black Scout

Halfway between Burnley and Todmorden the hills close in to form the Cliviger Gorge. A line of crinkle-cut cliffs and rocky bluffs, collectively known as Thieveley Scout, look down on the woods and fields of the valley. It is an inspirational sight, and one at which this circular walk takes a closer look before tackling the moorlands above. Views are wide and largely unrestricted, and there is a strange mixture of the rural and the urban, past and present.

Distance:
6 miles/10km

Height gain:
1,310ft/400m

Walking time:
4 hours

Start/Finish:
GR875286. Limited car parking in the village. There is a large roadside lay-by about 200yds/m along the road towards Todmorden.

Type of walk:
Moderate to hard with steep climbs over rough, peaty moorland. Suitable for reasonably fit walkers.

Take the southbound unsurfaced lane by the bus stop 50yds/m north of the Ram Inn. This was once the old road to the now demolished Holme Chapel Station. It heads across the fields of the Cliviger Gorge directly towards the cliffs of Thieveley Scout and threads under a tunnel beneath the railway – the site of the old station.

Leave the track short of Buckley Farm for a narrow signposted footpath to the right, which zigzags through Buckley Woods with the thickly wooded mossy ravine of Black Clough falling away to the right.

The next section is a delightful climb out of the valley giving ever-widening views across East Lancashire towards Pendle Hill. Cross the stile at the exit of the woods and climb south-south-west on a narrow path up steep reedy flanks to the ruin of Thieveley Farm (GR874278, not named on maps).

The farm was once a popular bank holiday venue for the weavers of Burnley and Nelson, who would have caught the train to Holme Chapel Station and walked up. The entertainment would have been provided by cricket matches, hand-cranked roundabouts and swing-boats. The 16th-century farmhouse was demolished in the 1930s – a victim of the demise of upland farming.

Go through the top gate above the ruins and head south-west at the edge of a deep clough to the prominent rocks of Dean Scout.

The rocks offer a fine viewing perch down the length of the Cliviger Gorge, where the gritstone cliffs of Thieveley Scout look across to the white wind turbines of Warcock Hill. Strangely the gorge consists of two valleys separated by a short saddle of land beneath the Scout. Both are Calder valleys. One River Calder flows through Lancashire into

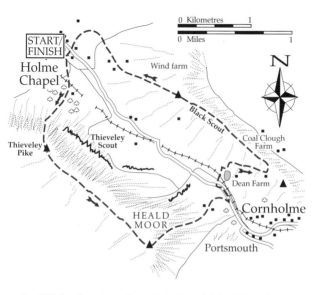

the Ribble; the other through industrial Yorkshire before joining forces with the Aire, near Castleford. Stoodley Pike guards the Yorkshire Calder valley towns, which from this vantage hide beneath the lower hill slopes.

In a final pull to the summit, Thieveley Pike, the route heads south across an area of disused opencast coal mines where it crosses an old flinted road.

Grass has now cloaked the scars but every so often there are rumblings in the press about re-opening them.

The summit, crowned by a trig point, offers wide views of Pendle Hill and the industrial towns of East Lancashire. Across the rolling green hills between the Ribble and the Aire the Craven Hills, including the instantly recognisable peaks of Pen y Ghent and Ingleborough, skim the horizon. Yet it is Black Hameldon and Boulsworth Hill that capture the attention. Their sullen gritstone-capped summits overlook wild expanses of stark moorland, where biscuit-coloured grasses and tussocks dappled with dark peaty runnels are punctuated by the odd glimmering blue lake. In the opposite direction Thieveley's western flanks, known as Deerplay Moor, decline gently into Rossendale which slinks away between the hills and pylons to the industries of Bacup and Rawtenstall. On most days the distance and the atmospheric haze soften the scene to pastel hues enabling the factories and warehouses to blend with the woods and lower pastures.

Thieveley Pike was one of a network of beacon hills where fires were lit to signal urgent news. Blackstone Edge was its southern neighbour and Pendle Hill, its northern counterpart.

Cross the stile over the ridge fence a few yards from the trig point. A rutted track veers south-east, veering away from the fence to head across the ridge towards Heald Moor, passing old mine workings at the saddle between the two.

At Heald Moor's top, a Burnley Way sign directs the route north-east on sheep tracks descending the fellsides. Aim for a dip in the drystone wall at the edge of the moor below: the dip marks the position of the stile.

Pleasant views into the valley develop as Beaver Clough deepens to reveal the terraces, factories and mill chimneys of Portsmouth and Cornholme, which are hemmed in by steep, partially wooded hillsides. Portsmouth was named by an old sailor who settled in these parts.

Beyond the stile the path meets a stony track. Turn left and follow it downhill to a gate to the left of an old ruin. Go through the gate and follow another track, descending north-north-east across bracken-clad pastures before veering to the right to join a bull-dozed road. Descend along this into the forest to meet the Burnley road at GR898265.

Turn left along the busy road and follow it for about 300yds/m. Leave it for a farm road that circumvents the small lake to Dean Scout Farm. At the farm, scale the ladder stile to the left and climb on a green road that zigzags up the grassy hillsides, passing another small lake and some ruins to reach a nick in the Black Scout ridge.

Keep to the right of the wall and turn left along the ridge, where you can see the wind farm in all its glory. On reaching a sub-station 2km/1^1/$_4$ miles along the ridge, go over the stile and follow the opposite side of the wall. After passing beneath a line of pylons the wall turns left leaving the path in an open field that declines into the valley. Turn half left, descending along a line of reeds that have obscured the sunken path. Cross another stile at the far end, then resume a north-westerly course on the north bank of a dyke to join a green farm road, which leads to a stony farm track. Turn right along the track (but ignore the nearby uphill zigzag) and pass in front of the farmhouse (GR881285).

The path continues beyond a stile at the end of the track and traces the eastern perimeters of delightful mixed woodland, descending to cross Green Clough (GR880287) on a footbridge. Now climb the opposite banks on a narrow path through bracken, passing a small coal mine to the right. The path returns to the edge of the woods and traverses two lofty fields to reach a walled track descending south-west back to Holme Chapel.

18 Inchfield Moor and Freeholds Top

Inchfield Moor, at 1,488ft/454m, is the highest of the hills that surround Todmorden, and offers wide vistas of the Rossendale and Calder valleys, Stoodley Pike and Blackstone Edge. Before hitting the heights this route discovers an attractive little glen complete with some picturesque waterfalls. It descends through a desolate area once crowded with mines and miners' smallholdings. Now it is empty (except for the cattle), left for the walker to examine the skeletons of the past.

Distance:
7 miles/11km

Height gain:
980ft/300m

Walking time:
4 1/4 hours

Start/Finish:
Gorpley Clough Foot, 1 mile/1.5km west of Todmorden on the A681 Bacup Road. GR917237. Enclosure for a few cars.

Type of walk:
A moderate moorland walk with good paths through the initial woodland stages, but more difficult going on the moors.

This narrow, wooded dene bites deep into the steep grassy slopes of Inchfield Moor. A little footpath (signposted "Gorpley Clough") climbs from the road-side by the side of a timber yard. A well-constructed staircase of stone takes the path to the streamside. Cross the stream on a little wooden footbridge and climb on the path, which wends its way past a couple of pretty waterfalls, both in shady bowers decorated by fern, campion and ragwort.

The path recrosses the stream and climbs out of the dene to a gate by North West Water's treatment plant, which lies beneath the huge Gorpley Reservoir dam. Turn right to follow the stony track, which circumvents the plant and climbs beneath pylons to a T-junction west of Gorpley farm. Turn left along a walled lane for a short way but leave this when it veers left to descend to another farm. Instead maintain a west-south-westerly direction by crossing the primitive stile by a gate and continuing across fields above the farm.

To the south, the waters of the Gorpley Reservoir, built to supply Todmorden, lie under the steep green lower slopes of Inchfield Moor, where a line of electricity pylons slices the scene into two.

Keep to the same contour line until a cart track from the farm climbs to join the path at a five-bar gate. Follow the track until it disappears in tussocky cow pastures at the edge of the moors. A faint track is beginning to be ingrained on to the ground, but it is spasmodic and confused by the odd sheep track. The going improves slightly beyond the crossing of the infant Gorpley stream. The route to the ridge is trackless; be content to aim for the mine on the horizon.

Cross the cinder track, which once served the local mines. A footpath sign points the way uphill to a ladder stile on ridge wall. A small pool on the other side of the wall lies surrounded by cotton grass. It can be quite a spectacle on a sunny July day. Turn left and follow the wide ridge.

Views from the middle are restricted to distant hilltops, but they improve on the approach to Freeholds Top where the ridge narrows. To the west the busy industrial towns of Bacup and Rawtenstall cram into the Rossendale valley, which threads between a complex of rounded hills. Notable amongst these is Cowpe Moss, whose eastern slopes have been defiled by a vast area of quarries and mines.

The right of way, known as Limers Gate, continues south-east along the ridge before diverting to the high southern flanks. Inchfield Moor's summit, known as Freeholds Top, lies slightly to the east of the ridge wall – a stile allows access.

A concrete trig point marks the summit. Next to it, cotton grass grows in profusion round a shallow circular pool. Eastern panoramas include the shapely escarpment rising to the Stoodley Pike monument. This viewing platform is just high enough to see the Warland and Light Hazzles Reservoirs on the lofty Langfield plateau and the serrated craggy summit of Blackstone Edge to its south.

Return to the Limers Gate path and follow it south. It becomes a walled grassy track and returns to the ridge. The walls open out to form a narrow field at a moorland col between Freeholds Top and Hades Hill. A step stile at the top left hand corner of the field (GR904206) gives access to the path of descent into Ramsden Clough.

The Ramsden Clough Reservoir is tucked beneath steep grassy slopes while Inchfield Moor's sleek slopes lie to the left. Beneath them sad ruins pepper the high fields –

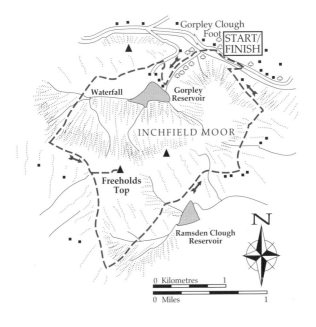

perhaps the last remnants of miners' smallholdings, or upland farmers who looked for pastures new in the valley towns, or America.

The good path descends to the remains of an old pit, where it becomes a rutted track winding down towards the reservoir. The rutted track becomes a stony track that used to be the bed of a railway carrying coal from the mines at Trough Edge to the valley. Follow its course, parallel to the reservoir and beneath the ruins of Coolam. On reaching some terraced cottages by a reedy pool, a signpost shows the way north across Inchfield Pasture.

In summer the prolific cotton grass covering the high moorland plateau superbly embellishes the day's best view encompassing Stoodley Pike, now boldly fronted with the cliffs of Langfield Edge. Opposite, the barren gritstone edges of Black Hameldon overlook the high hamlets of Cross Stone and Hole Bottoms, which lie on a verdant shelf above the Calder valley.

The old track, paved in places by slabs of millstone grit, traverses the lofty moors before meeting a good old-fashioned farm lane with two rutted wheel tracks and grass in the middle. Follow it north-west, ignoring the route to Gauxholme to the right.

As the track descends the valleysides, Todmorden comes into view. Its Victorian houses, mills, factories, viaducts, railway and canal make up a fascinating tapestry of rural and urban landscapes.

The pointed escarpment of Todmorden Moor soars further into the sky with every footstep. The last farm, Hollow Dene, has a lovely garden. In summer the air will be scented with rose and honeysuckle.

Beyond Hollow Dene a narrow Tarmac lane doubles back, emerging from behind an old mill and tall brick chimney to the Bacup Road just 200yds/m south-east of the starting point.

19 Cowpe Moss from Rossendale

In the past Rossendale's southern hills were ravaged by industry. Their streams were harnessed to power mills and quarrymen slashed the slate. Nowadays industry has retreated to the valleys leaving a legacy of crumbling slate walls and slag heaps. Walkers can now follow in the footsteps of the miners, weavers and quarrymen from their valley towns, or they can trace the ancient pack-horse trails to the tops and enjoy that bracing air and fine views of distant hills. This route captures the essence of Rossendale – it is not beautiful, but somehow its presence comes through that austere and broken skin.

Distance:
5 miles/8km

Height gain:
820ft/250m

Walking time:
3 hours

Start/Finish:
Car park and picnic site above Waterfoot.
GR834214.

Type of walk:
Moderate walk on quarry tracks to the high moors.

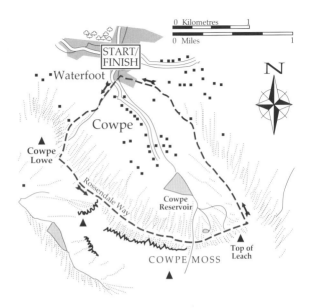

Turn right out of the car park along a farm lane that climbs south-west past several small reservoirs.

Almost from the start there are views back to the Rossendale valley. In spring there is a greenness about the place that belies its nearness to industry.

Buttercups and daisies in the surrounding meadows splash vivid colour into the scene. The lane is shaded by trees, horse-chestnut, beech and sycamore, while ahead the sullen moors loom large on the horizon.

The track squeezes between two houses with mock-Georgian windows and veers left. Now a grassy rutted track, it rakes up the moorland slopes east of Cowpe Low and wiggles to the right to avoid a shaley miniature ravine (GR828207).

Do not be tempted on to the path directly up Black Hill, which in recent times has undergone a moorland regeneration scheme, but continue south-west to a junction of tracks. Turn left here on a stony one which climbs steadily to Black Hill's western slopes.

The track south of Black Hill is strangely straight in the early stages, lending a sort of geometry to the landscape – a geometry accentuated by the pyramidal heaps of grass-cloaked spoil from the slate mines and quarries.

As the track rounds the corrie it runs through an area where quarrying has left rock faces resembling squat cliffs. In winter they are dark and dripping with water from surrounding peat moors. In summer they pale, becoming dry as a bone, home to ferns and the odd intrepid bush. The Cowpe Reservoir fully comes into view topped by the waters of the Cragg High Level Tank, which is surrounded by dark castellated stone walls.

Ignore all paths diverging to the left at this stage and follow the main track veering gradually to the right. At GR852197, close to some tall gateposts, the track meets the Rooley Moor road that will eventually be the route of descent. But first it is best to head south along it in order to scale the true summit of Cowpe Moss, Top of Leach. Two rows of gritstone slabs now form the basis for the old road. On reaching the commemoration stone for the Rossendale Way, abandon the track for a faint path climbing to the summit.

Here the view is mapped out on a brass plaque mounted on a stone pillar that was erected to commemorate the new borough of Rossendale, formed in 1974. Bowland, Pendle Hill, Ingleborough and Pen y Ghent span the northern horizon above Rossendale. To the south the view is of more sombre moorland clad with cotton grass, declining to the wide plains of Greater Manchester. Scattered tower blocks poke through the distant haze and you might pick out a few glimmering reservoirs. Hollingworth Lake's rounded shores are framed to the east by Blackstone Edge backed up by the Saddleworth hills. On a clear day, the Clwydian Hills and Snowdonian mountains will feature in the south-west. A glance to the east reveals the hideous scars of the Britannia Quarries.

Return to the Rooley Moor road.

Some walkers may wish to visit the cobbled surface of the road which lies a little to the south. The cobbles were laid by workers made redundant by the cotton famine of the mid-19th century. The cotton famine was brought about by the reliance on the United States for the raw materials and the termination of supplies during their civil war. In an early form of the Welfare State, the British government offered those out of work alternative employment at "fair and reasonable wages".

On returning to the junction at GR852197, descend north down the Rooley Moor road to a farmhouse by a radio mast (not shown on the Outdoor Leisure Map). Turn left in front of the farmhouse and over the primitive stile into the field beyond. A rutted track develops into a deep grassy channel which veers to the right. After going through a gate the track meets a Tarmac lane by a small enclosed reservoir (again not shown on the OL map).

Continue the descent along the lane, which degenerates into a stony track. Turn left as the track turns sharp right, tracing the perimeter of the field to the housing estate. Follow the estate road and turn first left along a street of terraced houses. It emerges almost opposite the lane to the car park.

20 Knowl Hill and Cowpe Moss

Knowl Hill is the first true summit on a beeline north from the centre of Manchester, so it is not surprising that it gives the finest bird's-eye view of the city. Pick out the famous buildings, scan the far blue horizons across wide plains – all laid out on this journey over cloth cap working hills.

Distance:
11 miles/18km

Height gain:
1,010ft/340m

Walking time:
5-6 hours

Start/Finish:
Owd Betts public house by the Ashworth Moor Reservoir (GR830160).

Type of walk:
A moderate walk on rough moorland paths and stony tracks.

Suitable for reasonably fit walkers, but **not recommended in poor visibility.**

Plenty of parking on large roadside lay-by opposite the pub.

A footpath signpost to the south of the Owd Betts public house points the way east across the moors. This route disregards the right of way shown on the map (indistinct underfoot due to lack of use) and follows the clearly defined and well-used path heading directly to the top of Knowl Moor.

From the summit trig point the wide conurbation of Manchester and its satellites sprawl across the flatlands, framed by Winter Hill and the main Pennine range around Blackstone Edge.

Head north-north-west from the summit on a faint path across peatlands and wet, rushy moors. A dyke, named on the map as Man Road Ditch, soon accompanies the path. Cross the fence straddling the moors to the south of Higher Hill on a step stile and continue to the empty hollow and breached dam at GR834186, which is marked on maps as a reservoir. Cross it with care.

To the north of the dam the route joins the Rossendale track, which leads north-east to a stile next to a large gate. A Rossendale Way (RW) sign points the way as the path enters a little ravine, which opens out to reveal a small reservoir, tightly tucked into steep grassy hill slopes. Follow the wide track, which joins in from the reservoir, descending to the east of Scout Moor with Cowpe Low's summit directly ahead.

Turn right (at GR828203) along another stony track that doubles back south-east across a vast area of disused quarries.

In contrast to the dramatic desolation, Cowpe Reservoir nestles in verdant, flower-decked fields next to a mill complete with tall chimney.

Ignore all paths diverging to the left and follow the main track to GR852197, close to some tall gateposts, where it meets the Rooley Moor Road. Turn right along the road to a Rossendale Way commemorative plaque where a short detour on a grassy path climbs to Top of Leach, which at 1,555ft/474m is the highest point of the day.

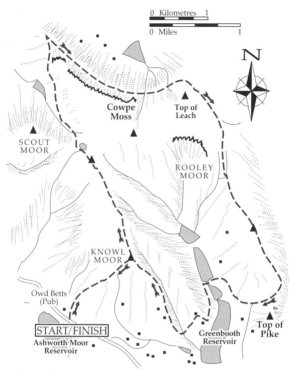

The brilliant views, extending to Pendle Hill and Ingleborough, are mapped out on a brass plaque set in a concrete pillar near to the trig point.

After retracing footsteps, continue along the Rooley Moor Road, which becomes a cobbled highway descending grassy moorland. This is the Cotton Famine Road.

On the descent, Manchester lies beneath your feet, bordered by the pale blue outlines of Blackstone Edge, the

Peak District and, on a clear day, the mountains of North Wales. A hollow develops to the right, its acid pastures and broken-down walls declining to the Naden Reservoirs.

Turn right on a track (signposted "To Greenbooth") and running parallel to some pylons. It passes beneath the radio mast of Hunger Hill to meet a lane, which swings to the right to its termination above the Greenbooth Reservoir. Greenbooth village was sunk beneath these waters.

Go over the stile by a gate and take the road to the Naden Middle Reservoir dam (the second most northerly of the four reservoirs). Cross the dam and turn left along the reservoir shores. At a solitary stone gatepost by a couple of sycamores (GR854158), turn uphill past a ruined barn to reach East Knowles Farm. Cross the stile, which is broken and slightly difficult, turn right along its drive, and take the right fork to Knowl Farm (GR848159). Go through a gate at the far end of the farmyard and beneath a lean-to canopy to a stile at the southern perimeter of a fairly new wood.

The path continues north, squeezing through the trees and out on to the moors. A grassy groove guides progress across rough terrain north towards Knowl Moor. On reaching unenclosed land, turn left. Convenient sheep tracks trace the right of way parallel to the stone wall on the left to meet the outward route south-west of Knowl Moor where a return should be made to the reservoir and into the "arms" of Owd Betts.

21 Around Watergrove

There are two waymarked trails around Watergrove – the Watergrove Trail and the slightly longer Hades Trail. The route described here is longer than both, spending more time on the moorland skyline. It is a walk through history, discovering old pack-horse trails and the ruins of 17th-century farmhouses that were obliterated to make way for the reservoir.

Distance:
5 1/2 miles/9km

Height gain:
720ft/220m

Walking time:
3 hours

Start/Finish:
Watergrove Reservoir
Car Park. GR912176.

Type of walk:
Old farm roads and
moorland paths. It can be
a little muddy after rain.
Good map reading and
compass skills required.

**Not recommended in
poor weather conditions**

The depression of the 1930s hit Lancashire hard, particularly the cotton industry. In the Rochdale area the local authority decided to put their unemployed men to work on the construction of a new reservoir in the high hollow of Watergrove. The village, which would have to go, supported a population of over two hundred, had two pubs, forty houses, a chapel, a smithy and two mills. All were demolished for the new excavations along with the farmhouses higher up the valley.

In 1938, after eight years and five million man hours of hard labour, they completed the dam and finally they sank old Watergrove beneath 720 million gallons of water. Set into the reservoir wall are a number of date stones and other artefacts that were rescued from the demolished dwellings. Today windsurfers scud across the waters and across the imaginary rooftops.

Go through the kissing gate at the eastern end of the car park and climb the steps to the top of the dam. Across the waters of the reservoir the smooth topped moors of Brown Wardle, Hades and Rough Hill spread across the skyline. Go through the gate at the end of the dam and follow the stony track north to a T-junction of tracks (GR912181).

Follow the wide stony track (signposted "To Hollingworth"), climbing north-east by some newly-planted trees. It swings right, goes through a five-bar gate in a castellated stone wall and follows the wall south-east. By now the path has lost most of its stones and has become a sunken dirt track. When the wall veers left, a small rush-ringed lake comes into view. So does the larger more distant Hollingworth Lake, which basks among town houses and low hills with the stony slopes of Blackstone Edge rearing up behind.

As the track comes level with the southern shores of the little lake it veers left by an old wall. Leave it here for a little path that doubles back north to climb a grassy spur. As it gains height the path gains confidence to become a rutted grassy track with drainage

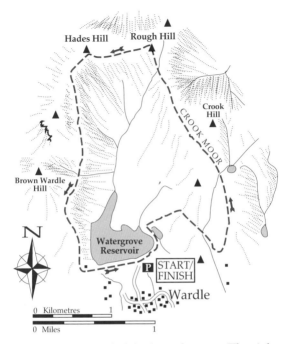

ditches. Take the left fork high up the spur. (The right fork passes close to an unnamed lake beneath Turn Slack Hill to end at a beautifully built stone shelter that has been in view from the start of the path.)

The correct path narrows again and winds through the grassy spoil heaps of old mines, passing to the left of and beneath the previously described shelter. Briefly, it traces a stone wall high on the slopes of Crook Hill, but when the wall turns downhill the route maintains its north-westerly direction across the moors and above some mining spoil heaps – just a sample of the hundreds scattered across the moorland combe and hillslopes.

The route approaches the head of the combe with Rough Hill and Hades Hill closing in on the rough lower pastures. A substantial track cuts across the path by a couple of stone cairns. This is the Long Causeway, an old packhorse route between Burnley and Halifax. Keep straight ahead, on a path descending slightly towards Higher Slack Brook. It turns right to ford the stream uphill at GR914200.

Ignore the busier track raking across the southern slopes of Rough Hill, but climb on the one north to the grassy moorland col to the east of the hill. A short but stiff trackless climb leads to the gravelly summit, where a new view to the sleek escarpment of Freeholds Top unfolds.

A faint path continues to Hades Hill where Rossendale appears for the first time. Follow the series of Rossendale Way posts amid a confusion of quarrying tracks to the rush-ridden col beneath the quarry-massacred top of Middle Hill. Clay, boulders and pits are everywhere, making a quick exit essential.

Descend south-south-east on faint track along the high slopes of Middle Hill to pass an old shaft and some spoil heaps. A broken down stone wall joins in from the left and keeps the route company past several ruins, which are, in general, surrounded by a few sycamores. None of the old farms is named on the maps but they are marked on the ground by wooden commemorative plaques.

A couple of tracks climb to the right, trying to lure the walker back to the tops, but stay low to capture the ghostly reminders of old Watergrove. Beyond the ruins of Middle Hill Farm the path becomes choked with rushes. Go though a gap in the wall to follow the other side. Another gap, 20yds/m later, allows access back to the proper line. The narrow path fords Long Shoot Clough then climbs out to Broad Ing. A sign, H8 (Hades Trail Point 8), highlights the left fork to be taken. It follows the line of a sunken, rush-filled walled track to the High Wardle Farm complex, where piles of slate and stone and a few gateposts are all that remain.

From High Wardle, aim for the tall waymarking post to the south and follow the path across pastures, keeping parallel to the sunken lane on the left. Turn left to cross a wooden stile on to a green lane, tightly enclosed by the walls. On reaching a stand of trees the lane turns left then gradually veers south. On the approach to the new water treatment works, turn left across some levelled quarries to the Watergrove dam. Go through the gate, cross the overflow, and descend the embankment to the road, which climbs back to the car park.

22 Reddyshore Scout and Crook Moor

This walk follows centuries' old routes across the Pennines, some of which, like the Long Causeway and Reddyshore Gate tracks, are still well used and easy to follow, while others have returned to the moor. This is archetypal South Pennine country, where busy industrial valleys with 19th-century canals and railways vie for space with 20th-century roads. Once above the quarry-scarred hillsides the route takes to the windswept moors that stretch for many a mile to the next invisible industrial valley beneath the skyline.

Distance:
6 miles/10km

Height gain:
920ft/280m

Walking time:
4 hours

Start/Finish:
GR943194 on the Calderbrook Road. Parking in the adjacent lay-by or on roadside between here and the Steanor Bottom Road House.

Type of walk:
A short but serious undertaking outside the summer months. Only suitable for properly-equipped walkers experienced with both map and compass.

Not recommended in poor weather.

The cylindrical stone towers protruding from the trackside on the initial stages of the walk are the ventilation shafts of the Summit railway tunnel. The tunnel, nearly 3,000yds/m long and up to 100yds/m beneath the surface, was built in 1841 at a cost of £250,000. It was part of the Calder valley line, the first railway to cross the Pennines. In 1984, a fuel train caught fire while in the tunnel and the air shafts became chimneys of fire and black smoke.

Go through the gate at the start of the grassy track and climb steadily beneath the iron-stained gritstone crags of the Scout.

Views down the valley become wider after passing a cluster of sycamores. Looking down from here, the little hamlet of Warland is settled in a nick in the hillside. A few highly-coloured barges will probably be in moorings on the canal near a lovely whitewashed lock-keeper's cottage, which languishes beneath precipitous craggy slopes. Further north, beyond the crags of Lower Scout, the Great Bridestones, which cap the hillslopes above Todmorden, vie for attention with the white wind turbines of Coal Clough.

The track passes under a line of pylons. Beyond a stile, it narrows and turns left above a little hollow. Abandon it here for a track that rakes steeply up to the crest of the Scout to join a bulldozed road, part of the Reddyshore Gate packhorse route. Turn left along the old road and back under the pylons, then right to follow a sketchy path tracing a dilapidated wall across tussocky cow-trodden pastures. A partially-paved section of the path veers slightly away from the wall for a while to traverse some of the wettest ground preceding the stone-scattered slopes of Ferny Hill. The faint path heads south as the wall turns into Owler Clough. A rusting steel sheet (the bottom of a lorry) spans a dyke at GR937195.

A sparkling sheet of water, Hollingworth Lake, comes into view across the urban plains to the left and the path fades to become little more than a sheeptrack. Take the right fork on Allenden Hill: the left one descends to Calderbrook. It proceeds briefly along the edge of a pastured hollow before giving up the ghost in the rougher moor grasses.

Head west across the featureless moors, which can be wet but never marshy. The right of way sticks to high ground to the south of Great Hill. A useful land-mark does appear on reaching Foxstones Hill in the form of a fold in the hills ahead. This is the basin of the little reservoir beneath Turn Slack Hill and the route must keep to the north of it. Watch out for the pale grasses of a shallow-grooved track, which comes in from the right across the moors. It will cross three rushy, moss-surrounded streams before raking to the right (north-west) by a cairn to the summit of Crook Hill. This last raking hollow will be visible from a distance.

(NOTE: For anyone not strictly on line hereabouts, it is worth noting that there is a prominent circular shelter on the southern slopes of Crook Hill close to the previously mentioned little reservoir. A simple climb on the ridge from the shelter would bring the walker back to the correct line.)

Crook Hill's summit is topped by a small pile of stones. Views have opened up to include the Watergrove Reservoir, set in a wide bowl of high pastures, and the vast plains and cityscapes of Greater Manchester. Completed in 1938, the reservoir submerged Watergrove, a typical Lancashire village with cobbled streets, terraced houses, two pubs and a couple of mills. More rounded hills surround its hollow. Middle Hill has a quarry on its summit. The sides of Hades Hill and Rough Hill were scorched by moorland fires in 1995. The scars will heal and the hills will return to their biscuit colour but meanwhile they serve as a reminder of the damage a carelessly discarded cigarette can cause to our heritage.

Continue north-west along the ridge of Crook Moor to a crossroads with the Long Causeway, a well-defined old packhorse route linking Burnley and Halifax – a cairn marks the spot. Turn right along the old road which, in places, is paved with old causey stones. After straddling the moor it passes between tall gateposts in a stone wall and descends to the top edge of a cavernous hollow where it runs alongside a stone wall. The Cranberry Reservoir lies beneath the sullen northern slopes of Shore Moor, looking more like a bath tub than a lake. It overlooks some shaley clough-sides and some woodland, which enlivens the scene. After passing beneath a line of pylons the old road becomes a bulldozed track that descends to a five-way junction.

The most pleasant route from here to Walsden is by Ragby Bridge and down the wooded valley north of the river. Unfortunately a landslip near the old packhorse bridge has made the route extremely dangerous. In time a permissive bridleway may be engineered along the northern banks. Until that happens it is better to follow the track veering to the right past Inchfield Farm and descending to the Ramsden Road by a little mill pond.

The road sneaks past the Walsden Print Works and some other factories and follows the river to emerge on the main road by the Border Rose pub. Turn right along the road, passing the Waggon and Horses Inn before crossing to the other side.

Go down some steps at the far side of a cottage (GR937212) and cross a footbridge spanning a stream before carefully crossing the railway line. The path veers left along the edge of a field to join the towpath of the Rochdale Canal. Turn right along the towpath past the Lightbank and Sands Locks.

The surroundings are pleasantly rural and peaceful. Anglers more often than not will be fishing the rush- and iris-lined canal, and the attractive whitewashed lock-keeper's cottage spied earlier in the day from Reddyshore Scout looks even better from down here. It is dwarfed by Walsden Moor's soaring crag-fringed slopes.

Leave the towpath at Bottomley Lock for a Tarmac lane that passes some terraced cottages before climbing back to the Littleborough road. Turn left along the road for 50yds/m then leave it for a track on the other side, signposted to Calderbrook. Beyond the houses it becomes a partially-paved track, which initially fights its way though tall thickets of bracken, bramble and wildflower before veering left to cross a stony lane. Go straight ahead though the gate and on to a grassy track which climbs past another air shaft. There are some marshy stretches but most can be circumvented.

The outwards route is met beneath the pylons and there is just a short downhill section for a return to the start.

(NOTE: At the time of writing there are applications for new wind farms to be sited on hillsides to the north and west of Watergrove Reservoir. If passed, the schemes would necessitate the building of new tracks across the moors.)

CALDERDALE

In political reality Calderdale covers vast areas of urban sprawl, from the outskirts of Burnley to those of Bradford, and the bustling towns of Halifax and Sowerby Bridge. In this guide, however, Calderdale refers to the upland regions of the Calder and Ryburn rivers.

Hebden Bridge in the central regions is the self-proclaimed capital of Calderdale's tourist region. The town is a fascinating mix of rural and urban charm with row upon row of dusky four-storey terraces encircling the hillsides in perfect symmetry. Antique shops, cafes, hotels and inns fill the centre. The Rochdale Canal, usually decorated with colourful barges, flows through the town.

But it is the fine walking that makes Hebden Bridge special. The Calder itself is not beautiful. It is a narrow twisting valley in which houses, factories, a railway, main road, river and canal, all compete for space with the trees – it is just too hectic, though the canal towpath offers easy and pleasant returns to base.

The real beauty is in the wooded "deans" or "denes". Three of them radiate from the main valley: Hebden Dale, known locally as Hardcastle Crags, Crimsworth Dean and Colden Clough. Lovers of woodland walking will be in their element at Hardcastle Crags, which scythes through the moors to Widdop Gate. Crimsworth Dean is more open and has an attractive little waterfall at its head. It also offers good walking routes across the moors to Haworth and a climb to the bleak, windswept High Brown Knoll. Paths through the third valley, Colden Clough, climb to Heptonstall, an old weaving village with cobbled streets and 17th-century cottages huddled round a ruined abbey and a modern church. It is a smaller version of Haworth, and without the crowds.

On the opposite side of the valley, Stoodley Pike and the monument that borrowed its name tower above Todmorden, a proud but more austere town than Hebden Bridge. The Pike is the craggy northern outpost of a wide expanse of heather moorland on the main Pennine watershed. Almost plateau-like hereabouts it swells gradually to the summit at Holder Stones.

The southern end of the plateau is drained by the River Ryburn, whose pleasant valley joins the Calder at Sowerby Bridge. A couple of the walks from the Ryburn are listed in the next chapter but one of the finest short walks in the book is to the heather-clad Norland Moor, which overlooks the valley at Ripponden.

Calderdale paths are some of the best kept and best waymarked in the British Isles thanks to the forward looking Calderdale MBC who have worked closely with the Countryside Commission and major landowners. In 1978, the groups pioneered the Calderdale Way, a 50-mile long distance path around the borough. They have since introduced many new paths and access agreements, including ones to the summit of Great Manshead Hill above the Ryburn and across Turley Holes south-east of Stoodley Pike. This guide makes full use of the new paths.

23 Around Hebden Dale

Hebden Dale, sometimes referred to as Hardcastle Crags, cuts and twists its way through high moors north-west of Hebden Bridge. Bursting with trees, shrubs and wild flowers, it makes a fine entrée to the high moorland traverse that follows. This walk uses the Dean Gate permissive path across Wadsworth Moor. Being a grouse moor, it is subject to closure at times of high fire risk and on shooting days, which occur between August 12 and December 12. A red flag will be flying on such occasions.

Distance:
7 1/2 miles/12km

Height gain:
1,150ft/350m

Walking time:
3-4 hours

Start/Finish:
The Clough Hole National Trust Car Park, on the old Hebden Bridge to Nelson road. GR969297.

Type of walk:
A mixture of woodland tracks and high moorland paths.

The car park overlooks Hebden Dale, a heavily-wooded valley fringed by cow pastures and topped by heather moor.

Descend into the dean on a wide stony track by a lively stream, which cascades through the darkness of the trees. Turn left at the first junction of tracks, then left again down gritstone steps, to cross the bridge over Hebden Water by Gibson Mill.

The 200-year-old mill is one of the few remaining cotton mills in the area. Originally driven by a water wheel, it was converted to steam in the 1860s. After ceasing life as an active factory, it was transformed into a restaurant and dance hall with boating on the mill ponds In 1995, restoration began on the mill in celebration of the National Trust's Centenary, to put it to use as a visitor centre.

Turn left around the far side of the mill on a wide track, passing the old mill pond, often frequented by dippers, mallards and dragonflies. The track gradually climbs past Hardcastle Crags, large outcrops of millstone grit, camouflaged by vegetation.

Take the right fork in the tracks beyond the crags. It climbs out of the woods and on to pastureland, where it meets a lane linking the high hill farms of Shackleton and Wadsworth Moors. Turn left and follow its lofty course to the little hamlet of Walshaw Farm, part of the Savile Estate.

The twisting dean appears through gaps in the sycamores while the wide spread of moorland captures the horizon.

From Walshaw the route aims to leave the farmlands and head for the moors. It does so on a courtesy path climbing north on a walled track that turns left for New Cote Farm. Just beyond the turn, a signpost ("To Walshaw Dean") points north, and the path climbs a

grassy bank to continue along a cart track from New Cote, which passes some mixed woodland to reach the open moor beyond a stile.

The meandering broad track from here onwards is out of bounds – for shooters only. (It will recross the path slightly higher uphill before wandering off to the obscurity of the forbidden shooting areas.)

Instead follow a narrower path, Dean Gate, which

climbs the shoulder of High Rakes on Wadsworth Moor.

The tussocky moors are dappled with heather and bilberry, with bracken taking hold in the more shaded depressions. On reaching the top, Widdop Reservoir comes into view, shaded by the dark craggy slopes of Widdop and Hameldon. A little to their left, the two Gorple Reservoirs huddle beneath the sombre slopes of Black Hameldon and Shuttleworth Moor.

The little path descends into Walshaw Dean, an equally stark valley scything into the vast moors south of Boulsworth and with three reservoirs of its own. Beyond a couple of stone-built shooters' boxes it joins a shooters' track, which descends to the dam of the Middle Reservoir. Turn left and follow the permissive path along the southern shores of the Lower Reservoir (there may be slight diversions until late 1996 to facilitate Yorkshire Water's construction programme).

Cross the dam of the lower reservoir, then turn left along the paved road down the Alcomden valley. Take the left fork by a small plantation of spruce and follow a farm track down the narrowing stony-sided valley of Alcomden Water to the Nelson Lane.

Alcomden Water and Graining Water meet at its foot and each is spanned by a bridge, the former for travellers on foot. The latter conveys the old road between Hebden Bridge and Nelson.

Turn right to climb along the lane to the next bend, where a stile in the wall marks the start of a footpath heading west. It traverses crag-ridden, grassy slopes above the bluffs of Ridge Scout. Two little wooden footbridges can be seen below, spanning Graining Water and the outflow of the Lower Gorple Reservoir, whose huge grass-covered dam towers above. They will have to be crossed later, but to get to them, the path must first continue north to GR948317. Here it meets the flagged Pennine Way track, an old pack-horse route: the route will follow the Pennine Way for the next two miles across Heptonstall Moor.

The white building to the east is the Pack Horse Inn and those with a thirst could well take a break here.

Double back along the old flagged path down an attractive craggy ravine, which is attractively trimmed with bracken, rowan and hawthorn. On reaching the riverbanks, the path crosses the two previously mentioned bridges and climbs the steep grassy banks beneath the reservoir's dam to Gorple Cottages, which belong to the water company.

In the sixties, a former keeper was tragically killed in blizzard conditions – a reminder that hills can be harsh places for the inexperienced.

Continue south on a wide track beyond the cottages and through some tall iron gates. Once across a leat, the track climbs south towards Heptonstall Moor. Abandon it beyond a fence. A PW signpost points the way east, though the improved path is never in doubt.

Views across the expansive hollows of Gorple, Widdop and Walshaw are wide and airy, with subtle colour shifts from the pallid green of the thin pastures through the straw-coloured moorland sedges to the dark mantle of heather. As the path reaches the shoulder of Clough Head Hill, Heptonstall village comes into view, with its fine church perched proudly on lofty pastures. The neighbouring hill-tops are breached by the curving, wooded valleys of Hebden Dale and Crimsworth Dean. Beyond them and across the Calder valley, Stoodley Pike appears on the horizon.

The path comes to the edge of the moor at Clough Head, where a rugged ravine overlooks more gentle pastures, which in turn tumble into Hebden Dale. Go through the gate in the wall that circumvents the ravine and descend along a narrow path through lush grassy slopes to pass behind the ruins of a grand old farmhouse – narrow gates are strategically placed in the crosswalls. Where there are two gates, halfway down, take the one on the right.

Dilapidated walls now confine the path, the one on the left being elevated by a grassy bank. A couple of signposts highlight a crossroads of footpaths. The right of way, signposted to Hardcastle Crags, passes in front of Clough House Farm, but the farmer has offered a diversion though a gate to the right avoiding the farmyard on the eastern side. It rejoins his drive, which descends to the road directly opposite to the car park at Clough Hole.

24 High Brown Knoll

High Brown Knoll is a fine summit with sweeping views across the moors of West Yorkshire. It rises from the Crimsworth and Luddenden Deans and connects a vast ridge of moorland spanning 13 miles between Colne in the west and Ogden north of Halifax in the east. This splendid circular walk from Midgehole starts on the well-waymarked Calderdale Way paths through woodland, but abandons them for a course along the tops.

Distance:
5 miles/8km

Height gain:
1,115ft/340m

Walking time:
2-3 hours

Start/Finish:
The National Trust car park at Midgehole.
GR989292.

Type of walk:
A combination of woodland and wild moorland.

The large National Trust car park is sited where the ravines of Crimsworth Dean and Hardcastle Crags (Hebden Dale) meet and, as such, offers a pleasing woodland start.

Follow the path behind the public toilets ("To Pecket Well") and take the middle of three paths. The paved route, bound by broken-down drystone walls, climbs on a winding course through beech trees.

The Pecket war memorial, an obelisk reminiscent of the one on Stoodley Pike, stands high above on the brow of the hill.

After crossing a stream at Kitling Bridge (GR994294), the path climbs out of the dean to the village of Pecket Well, crossing first the A6033 road and then a minor road from Chiserley. Turn right along the minor road for 100yds/m where a Calderdale Way sign points the way east on a cart track to Far Shaw Croft Farm. A path to the left of the buildings then rakes north-east up the hillside to GR000293, where a walled track climbs to the open fells. Here the route parts company with the Calderdale Way, which veers right.

This route follows the grassy groove of an old quarry track north-east to Deer Stones Edge. Just below the edge, a ruined building and a cylindrical air shaft mark the site of a disused mine.

On reaching the summit plateau continue along the western edge of the grassy moor with views west across Crimsworth Dean to Hardcastle Crags. On Summer Rake Edge, a sketchy path heads north-east to High Brown Knoll's summit, but, providing visibility is good, the trig point will be in view, and making a beeline for it will present no problems.

Distant views from the summit are of panoramic proportions. To the west, across the shoulder of Shackleton Moor, the rough hills of Black Hameldon and Boulsworth Hill catch the eye, with the bleak Gorple and Widdop Reservoirs lying beneath their craggy slopes. Further south, on the opposite side of the Calder valley, attention is drawn

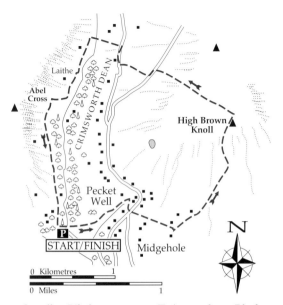

to Stoodley Pike's monument. To its south are Blackstone Edge and the GPO mast on Windy Hill. In the east, across pale grassy moors, a high sheet of water, the Warley Moor Reservoir, languishes below Nab Hill, a crag-interspersed escarpment, but the view here is marred by the new wind farm on Ovenden Moor.

Take the cairned Limers' Gate track from the summit, heading north-west across the plateau to Naze End, descending to the A6033 road. The strange contraptions to the north are those of Bradford University's laboratory.

The ground ahead sinks to Crimsworth Dean, which will act as a guide to the car park. Just to the south along the road, cross the step stile in a fence to the right, and descend across a tussocky field to a small gate, that lies in a hollow. After going through the gate, a narrow footpath between fences descends to the old Hebden Bridge to Haworth road at GR995312.

Turn right along the road for 100yds/m before turning left on a paved path that goes down to the banks of Crimsworth Dean Beck. Hereabouts in a shady, wooded niche the Lumb Hole waterfalls cascade down mossy rocks to a dark pool – a splendid old packhorse bridge overlooks the scene. Cross the bridge and follow the path that doubles back, climbing the opposite banks. Abandon the path by two stone gateposts for one traversing fields high above and parallel to the beck.

The prospect is an extremely beautiful one, with woodlands of pine, birch, and oak mingling with verdant pastures fringed by high moorland tops. The river gurgles and, more often than not, the sound of birdsong echoes through the valley.

Beyond a rustic cottage, the path climbs through a copse of pine to meet a high cart track that passes through mixed woodland and runs the length of the Dean to the car park. It is an easy-paced end to a beautiful walk.

25 Luddenden Dean

Luddenden Dean is one of the finest of Calderdale's side valleys, one that has not been commercialised. The roads are narrow and few, the population is sparse and the air is fresh. It is best explored on foot, and this route does just that, swooping from the heather-clad Warley Moor into the middle regions before climbing to the fringes of Midgley Moor. Jerusalem Woods at the valley bottom are beautiful and the stream that runs through them, clear. The walk climbs from this little oasis across fields and farms to the little hamlet of Saltonstall and back to the windswept moors. Note, however, that while the route across Midgley Moor follows rights of way, this is a grouse moor and shooting could occur between August 12 and December 12.

Distance:
6 miles/10km

Height gain:
1,000ft/305m

Walking time:
4 1/2 hours

Start/Finish:
Ovenden Moor by the wind farm. GR042308.

Type of walk:
Moderate walk with stiff climbs and descents.
A mixture of farm tracks, field paths and moorland.

The walk quickly turns its back on the white wind-mills of Ovenden Moor to go down Withens Head Farm's drive. Take the right fork after a few yards and follow the rutted track to the ruinous buildings of Slade.

Turn half right at Slade along the narrow path across fields to cross a dyke by way of a little plank bridge. The path follows a line of fence posts across the wet grassy moor. It keeps to the right of the prominent Rocking Stone then descends through heather, which takes a stronger hold on this side of the hill. The fields, woods and scattered cottages of Luddenden Dean gradually come into view and aspects improve. The path veers right, raking across Height Edge to meet the road by a castellated building with a fine archway.

The archway is the first of two gatehouses that belonged to the Castle Carr Estate, built for the Huddersfield wool entrepreneur, John Priestley Evans in 1850. Evans was killed in a train crash in 1868 and the estate changed hands. When John Murgatroyd sold it, the lavish main building was demolished – only the gatehouses remain.

The next footpath is dog-legged to the left and starts with a stile. It passes to the left of a cottage, over another stile and across fields. Look for a stile a few yards to the right of a five-bar gate that lies at the far end of the field, then descend further into the dean, keeping well to the left of a twisted hawthorn tree.

A little cart track takes over, zigzagging down steep slopes to the bottom road by the second castellated gatehouse. Turn right along the lane and across Luddenden Brook on Low Bridge.

The hard work starts by The Lowe Farm at the end of a lane. Go through the small gate on a footpath

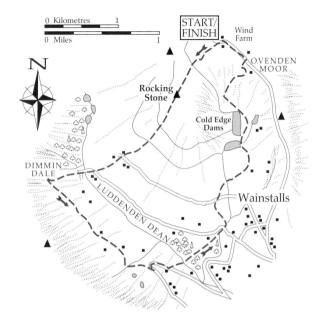

(signposted "Keelham Gate to the old town"). It climbs steep slopes of bilberry and bracken, keeping the fence to the right. A few sheep tracks wander off into the sweetest clumps of bilberry to the left, but the real path unrelentingly attacks the slopes, threading through tall bracken, then over bilberry, boulder and heather, to reach a cart track on Dimmin Dale Edge. Luddenden Dean is laid out to perfection, curving between the high heather moors from its beginning at Calderdale to its headland on Warley Moor. Turn left along the cart track but ignore the waymarking posts, which highlight the path descending back into the dean. This route continues along the rim of the moor alongside a sunken reedy track. Look out for a slight diversion to the right preceding a big rock: it avoids a very difficult crossing of the marshy beginnings of a stream (GR023286). After passing Ferney Lee Farm, the track ends.

Cross the stile on to a metalled lane that clings to the edge of the moor. Beyond Clough House take the left fork (the right fork is an unsurfaced cart track) which descends Dry Carr to Jerusalem Lane. Follow it downhill to a footpath (signposted "To Jerusalem Farm"). This descends into lovely woodland, on steps initially, with a couple of gates confirming the course to Wade Bridge. The one-arched bridge had to be rebuilt in recent times after the original was badly damaged by flash floods.

Climb out of the wooded valley on the upper of three paths to the right, then double back left at the first junction. The path out of the woods is signposted to Lower Saltonstall and climbs through an avenue of holly to a gate at the top edge – a footpath signpost for Saltonstall marks the spot. Climb on the well-worn path, which is punctuated by stiles in the drystone walls, with the stone cottages of Lower Saltonstall on the hillsides ahead and the mills at Wainstalls further to the right.

The path turns right beyond a stile by a more substantial wall, then left at a wall corner to pass between 17th-century stone cottages to the lane. Turn left along the lane for a few yards then squeeze through a gap in the wall opposite one of the cottages. Climb the steep fields with the wall to the left and up some derelict steps between a gap in a derelict wall. Here the route veers half left to a five-bar gate (GR039285). Turn right here on a faint rutted track running alongside a new fence. Maintain the same direction when the fence turns left and cross unkempt stony pastures to a small gate in the top right corner by the road. Turn right along the road then left over a stile. The clear path climbs the moor parallel to the outflow stream from the Leadbetter Dam to a footbridge by a weir, where it turns right to trace the top edge of some farm pastures.

Head north on the walled gravel track at the end of the path. After 300yds/m abandon the track at a stile in the left wall for a path across an old quarry. It joins a quarry track, but shortly leaves it for the grassy raised causeway along the Leadbetter Dam (marked as one of the Cold Edge Dams on Landranger maps). It continues along the Cold Edge Dam to rejoin the stony track by the jetty and shack belonging to the Halifax Water Skiing Club.

The landscapes north from here are sad. Beyond the "Private" sign of the skiers, rubble lines the track and the fields are choked with rushes, reeds and thistles. The farms lie abandoned and the moor ahead has been captured and imprisoned by those white windmills in the sky. In contrast, looking back is a revelation for the wide skies cap a fascinating mosaic of hills and plains. Black Hill can be recognised by its mast, while to its right, the dark, jagged top of Blackstone Edge caps the moorland expanse beyond the buildings of Halifax.

The track winds past the ruins of Haigh Cote. The marked path towards Slade Farm is unusable, crossing the most waterlogged tussocky fields imaginable. It is more prudent to continue along the track past the remains of Moorlands Farm. What a relief it is to get to the road. Quite by chance the Withens Hotel beckons on the opposite side.Walkers with a strong willpower, or bad timing, turn left along the road to return to the start (400yds/m).

26 Colden and Jumble Hole

Colden Clough and Jumble Hole Clough begin their lives on the high moors, gain momentum through the high pastured shelves surrounding Heptonstall and Blackshaw Head, respectively, before plummeting in tree-lined ravines into Calderdale. This walk seeks out cloughs and passes among the region's forgotten mill villages.

Distance:
8 miles/13km

Height gain:
1,000ft/305m

Walking time:
5 hours

Start/Finish:
Lay-by on the A646, at the foot of Colden Clough. GR985273.

Type of walk:
Moderate, but begins with a steep climb to Heptonstall. A typical Calderdale walk along causey paths, farm tracks, through woodland and over moor.

A narrow path begins behind some terraced cottages (Colden Close), at the edge of woodland and parallel to Colden Water. Beyond the cottages leave the path for one that doubles back through the woods then on to high fields. After 300yds/m it meets a well-worn path that has climbed from Hebden Bridge. Turn left and follow it up to a heather- and bilberry-cloaked craggy edge known as Eaves Rocks.

There are good views down both the tree-filled Colden Clough and Calderdale, whose roads, railways and canals weave through woodland and past mills and cottages beneath Stoodley Pike.

The path continues along the edge until it reaches some quarries where huge rock faces add a little shade to the scene. Climb the flight of steps to the left of the rocks and rake up the hillsides. On reaching the rim of the clough, the path passes some new houses on the outskirts of Heptonstall. Those wanting to visit the fascinating little village can go through the ginnel between the houses but they will have to retrace their steps.

Continue the route along the top of Eaves Wood – it follows the Calderdale Way for the next mile along the top of the clough. The path briefly dives into the shade of the trees before emerging on a surfaced farm road. Turn left along the road then leave it for a grassy path on the right-hand side just short of a substantial stone-built house, Lumb Bank, once home to Poet Laureate, Ted Hughes.

The path becomes partially paved with flags of mill-stone grit and passes a ruined farmhouse, (which, at the time of writing, looked as if it may be in line for renovation) and an old barn. Turn left beyond the latter on to an enclosed track descending towards the valley then right, following the Calderdale Way arrows along a partially-paved path across fields.

Cross a stile to the left just beyond a kink in the wall and descend to the top edge of Foster Wood. The path finally dips into the wood. Ignore the Pennine Way sign to the right for the moment, for a detour down to the water's edge by Hebble Hole Bridge, a little packhorse bridge that now conveys the famous long distance route. It makes an ideal lunch spot.

From the bridge climb the northern banks back to the Pennine Way sign and follow the line of the LDP on a walled path climbing north. It veers left in front of Goose Hey Farm (GR967285), then reverts to its former direction to the Blackshaw Head road through Colden village, a scattered weaving community that once had greater importance.

Continue north across the road on a path climbing another field to another country lane. Turn left here past High Gate Farm where they have a shop. The lane becomes unsurfaced and should be abandoned (at GR959290) for a farm track descending past the school, back into the Colden valley and a little wood. Turn right by a bridge to follow the lane towards Rodmer Clough taking the left fork to pass in front of the pleasantly-renovated cottage. Beyond it a track, the Moor Lane path, climbs to round the hillside into Noah Dale (ignore the left fork which is the drive of Top o' th' Hill farm).

In his book On the Tops around Todmorden, *Geoff Boswell mentions the possibility of hearing a lone bagpiper here. The landscapes have been getting bleaker – the fields of Noah Dale are the last reedy outposts before the transition to moorland.*

A wooden signpost ("To Dukes Cut"), points the way along a deeply rutted track that climbs uphill southwest to a junction with the Greenland Road track.

This is a place known as Three Gates End. Views have widened. Across the pastures of Noah Dale, the dark

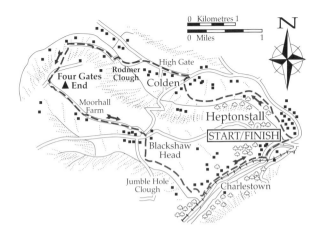

moors mottled with peat, heather and pale moor grasses swell to Black Hameldon in the west and the Haworth Moors in the east.

Climbing further, the track goes one better to reach Four Gates End, a moorland crossroads. Turn left here on the Moorcock Road, which soon becomes a stony path straddling Moorcock Hill.

Views south return, including Stoodley Pike, Blackstone Edge and Inchfield Moor. Nearer at hand the heather of Staups Moor catches the eye.

The Moorcock Road meets another stony track, Higher Back Lane, which leads east past several farms. Beyond a five-bar gate the surface changes to a grassy one, declining to a high lane at Blackshaw Head. Turn right along the lane to a T-junction by the Shoulder of Mutton pub and left for 200yds/m. Leave the road for a track (signposted "The Calderdale Way"), which descends south-west between a group of houses and across fields to Bullion Farm. Turn left to a gate by the cottage, which allows entry to more fields. Follow a wall to the next farm, which should be passed using a stile to the right of the farmyard.

Continue south across more fields and cross another stile to a track passing the house at Hippins. A signposted footpath to the left leads across fields and descends in a series of stone steps into the wooded Jumble Hole Clough (not named on maps). Cross the stream via a little footbridge and climb above its western banks. Do not be tempted by paths to the right, which climb out of the clough, but stay with the narrow path parallel to the stream. It passes the ruins of Staups Mill.

The shell of this huge water-powered cotton mill constructed in 1812 is hauntingly overgrown and shaded by woodland and the steep sides of the clough. It seems strange that in its heyday the whole place would reverberate to the sounds of the cotton-spinning looms and the hubbub of the workforce – today, only the rustle of the wind through the trees disturbs the silence.

The path is joined by a wide stony drive that has descended from hillside farms. It crosses the river by a weir and continues alongside the far banks, passing the remains of more mills. Further downstream the track passes another mill – this time used and complete with chimney. It continues to the right of the mill and beneath the railway to the busy A646. Turn left along the road, then right, past the garage and along the Pennine Way track, signposted to Callis Wood. It crosses the river to the canal towpath.

Leave the Pennine Way for the joys of the towpath which heads north-east to Stubbing Wharf. The exit point to the road is easy to find, right by the pub of the same name.

27 Todmorden Gritstone

This is one of the best walks in the book and typifies what is special about Calderdale. Forsaking the highest moorland, it climbs out of the busy valley to a pre-industrial revolution world set high on the hillside. The 17th-century cottages, some whitewashed, some of stone, are as beautifully kept as any Cornish village and their cultivated gardens are only matched by the surrounding fields of wild flowers. En route the walk visits crags and boulder fields of millstone grit culminating in the Great Bride Stones, the weirdest shaped rocks outside the Peak District. It is a complex route following many old farm tracks high on the valley sides. It is a good walk for late spring and summer when scenes will be embellished with blooming wildflowers.

Distance:
8 miles/13km

Height gain:
1,015ft/340m

Walking time:
5 hours

Type of walk:
A moderate walk, but with stiff climbs.

Start/Finish:
Lobb Mill Car Park and Picnic Site, east of Todmorden. GR956247.

The pretty tree-lined car park lies in the heart of the Calder valley where the railway, river, canal and road all squeeze through a narrow tract of land. The railway hereabouts goes over a viaduct then disappears through a tunnel in the hillside.

Follow the partially-cobbled path from the back of the car park. It quickly gains height as it zigzags through trees and heather.

Over the bracken-cloaked craggy slopes into the valley, the graceful curves of the railway line, canal and the busy road all lead to Todmorden, whose urban spread has been curtailed by the crowding hills. The soot-stained church perched high on the hillslopes is at Cross Stone, soon to be visited. Stoodley Pike dominates northern scenes, towering above the woodland, stark mills and tall chimneys.

When some farm buildings come into view, abandon the path and turn immediately left on a narrow path tracing the top edge of the hill. It meets a farm track at GR954248. Turn left off it almost immediately and on to a shrub-lined path that rounds the wooded ravine above Hill House. The path, which can be a little muddy outside the summer months, emerges at a country lane by Bean Hole head, a 17th-century cottage on the outskirts of Cross Stone. Follow the lane through the village, past the old church.

It is surprising and a little sad to find that on close inspection it is derelict – just a soot-stained shell. Apparently the church, rebuilt in 1835 has been subjected to landslip and is under threat of demolition. Among the charming white-washed cottages is the Berghof, an Austrian restaurant.

Turn right at the road junction at the eastern end of the village, then left on a track, which passes Todmorden's golf course and some old quarries. The

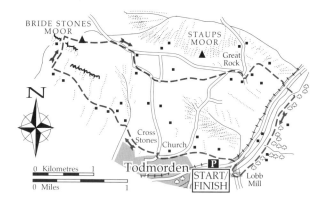

cragged mound of Whirlaw Stones fills the skyline and the route continues in this direction. The Calderdale Way joins in from the right above the deep hollow of Hole Bottom and the old cart track, now curbed with millstone grit in places, dives into the shade of oak trees. Cameos of Todmorden flicker in and out of their boughs.

Turn left along the path running north of East Whirlaw Farm. Heading west, it passes to the south of Whirlaw Stones across the open fells of Whirlaw Common. Those who want a closer look could easily make a detour on a prominent path.

Across the common, the track becomes paved with smooth slabs of millstone grit. This was an ancient packhorse road and, a few hundred years ago, would have been used to convey coal from Cliviger and lime from Clitheroe.

The old highway becomes enclosed again on rounding Whirlaw. Watch out for a narrow gap stile in the wall to the right, just beyond some old ruins. Go through it and climb the steep meadows. The track-less right of way continues over a stile in the top wall towards Bride Stones Farm, where a faint track appears. Follow it east to the jumbled rocks crowning peaty moorland.

The weirdest-shaped rocks, including one that resembles an upturned vinegar bottle, lie to the east of the trig point and are known collectively as Great Bride Stones. The name is possibly derived from the early British 'Breiad', which means mountain's edge.

If it is lunch time and you fancy refreshment, the Sportsman's Arms is only a short distance north and offers bar meals. This whitewashed inn on the Long Causeway road is haunted by a ghost named Rebecca.

Otherwise head east, crossing a stile to the Eastwood Road (GR938268). Turn right along the road and straight on at the next junction. About 300yds/m beyond the junction descend south on a stony track towards Higher Winsley Farm. Just short of the farmhouse turn left along a grassy track then right tracing a wall (R) south-east across a field.

A signpost ("To Lower Winsley Farm") by a stile at GR943263 points the way to the gap stile at the bottom of the field. From here a farm track leads to a lane. Turn left along the lane to a bend, then take the cart track in front of the cottage. It swings south and downhill before being quit for another track to the left. This continues east with superb views across the Calder valley to Stoodley Pike and the Langfield Edge.

In the middle regions the track becomes indistinct. Take the left of two gates then go across a stile by an electric fence and across a field on a narrow path, which dips to cross a small clough.

In summer the fields will be flecked with pastel blue harebell blooms and the verges with the pink flames of willowherb and foxglove.

Just beyond the clough, drystone walls converge and the path regains its cart track status to continue without incident to the lane at GR957263. Turn left along the lane then right at the T-junction to reach a huge faulted slab of gritstone known as the Great Rock. Being so close to the road it has attracted would-be stonemasons, who have openly declared their amorous intentions to the world.

Leave the road at the corner beyond the rock to follow yet another farm track. Take the first track on the left, signposted for Roundfield Farm. It heads north-east to the edge of Jumble Hole Clough, a deep, partially-wooded ravine (named Dean Delph on current maps). Leave the track for a rutted path that arcs to the right past some heather-bound crags.

Views down the Calder valley have opened up to reveal Hebden Bridge. From this angle the town appears to be under threat of being overwhelmed by the spread of oak, alder and birch. As ever Stoodley Pike's monument over-looks the scene.

Take the left fork as the new track splits just before reaching a small cottage. The path, which can be a little overgrown with grasses and wild flowers in summer, is surrounded by bilberry and bramble and bounded to the right by a drystone wall. After passing the last crumbling remnants of a farm building, it meets a tall crosswall at the edge of woodland. Turn left and follow a grassy path (still overgrown) that zigzags into Jumble Hole Clough itself, passing a cluster of cottages and Mulcture Hall to reach the railway. Turn right on the path alongside the railway, then left across a footbridge to cross over to the busy road.

Within a short distance the scene has changed from rural to urban for across the road there are red brick factories.

Turn right passing two or three of them until a short lane allows access to the canal. The track first crosses the River Calder, which runs alongside, to reach the towpath. Turn right here. The towpath runs along a narrow strip between canal and river for a good stretch. It seems strange, but the canal has been better looked after and is more salubrious than God's creation.

When Cross Stone church comes into view on the hills to the right, it is not far to the end of the walk. Abandon the towpath at the Lobb Mill Lock where a lane climbs back on to the main road opposite the railway viaduct. It is just 100yds/m west of the start.

28 Stoodley Pike from Cragg Vale

The climb from Cragg Vale is one of the more obscure ways to Stoodley Pike, but it is a pleasant way, climbing from the sylvan glen known locally as Bell Hole Clough. After sneaking up the quiet side of the Pike the route traces the magnificent escarpment's edge to Withens Gate. It descends by an ancient corpse road to the reservoir where it picks up a new and exhilarating permissive moorland route along Turley Holes Edge.

Distance:
8 miles/13km

Height gain:
900ft/275m

Walking time:
4 ½ hours

Start/Finish:
Clough Foot, Cragg
Vale. GR008246.

Type of walk:
Moderate: farm tracks.

Roadside parking for
cars.

A surfaced farm lane (signposted as a footpath) descends between two cottages to Clough Foot Bridge, spanning Cragg Brook, an attractive tree-enshrouded stream.

Ignore the riverside footpath to the right, but continue on the lane climbing out of the valley. After passing Lower Cragg Farm, leave the lane, now unsurfaced, for an overgrown sunken track running parallel. The two rejoin at a five-bar gate at Higher Cragg Farm.

By now views to the right across the wooded combe, known as Bell Hole Clough, extend across Mytholmroyd to Midgley Moor. The modern white windmills of Ovenden Moor appear on the horizon.

Pass in front of the farm buildings and continue along the farm track. At GR003246, by two five-bar gates, abandon the lane for a signposted footpath to the left. The sunken track runs parallel to a more defined dirt track on the other side of the fence, before swinging left to climb south-west to a gate on the edge of the open moor.

Go through the gate and turn right along a stony moorland track that traces the top of the farmland, passing Keelham Farm on its way to Bell House.

Bell House is a remote farmhouse with a dark history. Here was the home of "King" David Hartley, leader of the Cragg Vale Coiners, an infamous band of 18th-century counterfeiters. The coiners would clip the gold from the edges of Spanish and Portuguese coins (both legal tender in England at that time) before putting them back in circulation. They melted the clippings into a stone mould to manufacture more coins, which, in those days, would be hand-pressed and easy to counterfeit. Hartley became a local hero, but everything went wrong when William Deighton, a Customs and Excise man, who was hot on their trail, was found brutally murdered. Although David Hartley was arrested for the murder, the police could find insufficient evidence for a trial to take place. However, the intense pressure for a conviction of some kind led to

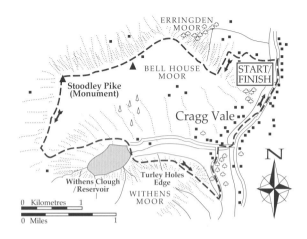

statements from number of the gang indicting their leader. In 1770, Hartley was tried, found guilty of counterfeiting and hanged at York. His body was buried in the graveyard at Heptonstall.

When the track veers right for Bell House, leave it for a paved path heading north-west round the head of Bell Hole. The gritstone flags give up on some very sticky moorland, and, outside the summer months, it requires nifty footwork to avoid the worst of it.

The right of way beyond Bell Hole is trackless so head west across the grassy moorland to pick up the wall corner at GR988248. Here an old grassy road known as Dick's Lane continues near the edge of the moor. Stoodley Pike's monument rises like a rocketship from the turf in views ahead. A wooden signpost marks the start of the lane's enclosure by stone walls. When they open out by a plantation of pine and spruce follow the course of the wall on the right – Stoodley

Pike will be straight ahead. The Pennine Way joins the path from a ladder stile in the wall to the right and the route becomes more prominent as it climbs to the obelisk.

Having surveyed the views of Todmorden, continue along the Pennine Way path, which is now a sandy track though gritstone boulders and cotton grass. Langfield Edge curves round, framing the chequered fields of Lumbutts and Mankinholes on a high shelf above the Calder valley. If it is afternoon Lumbutts' two small reservoirs will be glistening beneath the hillslopes.

The path passes an area of old quarries before dropping down to a pass known as Withens Gate. An old paved corpse road linking Mankinholes and Sowerby straddles the moor. Turn left along it and go through a gate in the ridge wall. A stone on the left, marked "Te Deum laudamas" (we praise thee O Lord), is a sacred point on the old corpse road where bearers would rest the coffin.

A well-defined path that is part of the Calderdale Way (CW) descends half right alongside a substantial stone wall. Withens Clough Reservoir comes into view, cradled by Withens Moor, which is embellished by bracken and gritstone crags known as the Buck Stones and capped by heather-clad peat.

Turn left along the well-defined grassy track at Red Dykes (GR972229) – a CW waymark arrow marks the spot. The track, which soon becomes lined by reeds and rushes, runs parallel with the reservoir shores. Below it are some pine woods, while above the boulder-strewn moors swell to Stoodley Pike. The track tries to lose itself, kinking to the right twice before reaching the north-western corner of the woods. It then continues north-east to a junction at GR977232. Turn right here on a grassy track descending to the stony road by the reservoir shores.

Withens Clough Reservoir was completed in 1894 to supply water to Morley, but now it conveys its supplies to the Baitings Reservoir in the Ryburn valley via the Manshead tunnel. Its capacity is 293 million gallons.

Turn right across the dam's causeway, then left along a new permissive footpath tracing an old stone-built drain along steep bracken-clad slopes of Turley Holes Edge. Heather takes hold and the path narrows considerably. Down in the valley the cottages and tall terraces of Cragg Vale are huddled between forest and hill slope, but the church is out of sight.

The drain gives up the ghost and sinks into a bed of reeds where the path veers right to pass above the top edge of Hove Yard Wood. The odd waymarking post guides the little path to a wooden signpost at GR000223 on Cove Hill. Turn left here to a gap in the wall by a tall gritstone gatepost. A stile in the fence beyond the gap gives access to a wide, rutted cart track that swings left to descend the hillside.

Go through a five-bar gate to the right on reaching some ruinous outbuildings. The track continues along the edge of a field to Higher House. Beyond another five-bar gate at the farm a stony lane descends across fields then beneath Hove Yard Wood. It meets the road opposite the Hinchcliffe Arms. Cross the bridge over Cragg Beck beneath the church and follow the signposted footpath between two rows of terraced cottages. A track through a field runs parallel to the river then climbs out past more terraces to the B-road just 800yds/m short of the start of the walk.

29 Stoodley Pike from the Calder

This circular walk follows the classic Pennine Way route to Stoodley Pike. Leaving the bustling Calder valley, it seeks the shade and the peace of Callis Wood before climbing to that dark obelisk on the skyline. Wide panoramas unfold in every direction – from the peaks of the Yorkshire Dales to the wild moors of the Peak District. The return route descends to Height Wood and finishes with a pleasant stroll along the Rochdale Canal.

Distance:
5 miles/8km

Height gain:
985ft/300m

Walking time:
3 hours

Start/Finish:
Charlestown
(GR972264), west of
the Woodman Inn.
Limited car parking by
Callis Bridge at the
start of the walk and on
nearby side-roads.

Type of walk:
A moderate circular
walk on tracks through
woodland to high
moorland.

**Take care not to block
gates or disrupt local
traffic.**

Charlestown, a sooty suburb of Hebden Bridge, lies in the narrow, steep-sided Calder valley, through which run the river, a railway, the A646 Halifax Road and the Rochdale Canal. It is an inauspicious start for a walk, but it offers a splendid approach to Stoodley Pike along the Pennine Way (PW).

A PW signpost points down the lane that crosses the River Calder, which rushes past on its rocky bed trying in vain to avoid the attentions of the nearby sewage works. Thankfully the lane turns its back on all this and crosses the tree-line Rochdale Canal on a typical, one-arched hump-back bridge. Brightly coloured canal boats liven up the scene.

Veer left on a good stony track that climbs past some terraced cottages into the shade of Callis Wood, where it zigzags beneath beech and hazel trees on a carpet of bluebells and wild garlic.

In retrospective views from this pleasant niche between the rounded knoll of Edge End Moor and Erringden Moor, the Calder valley seems more green, unspoiled and less grimy. It is more peaceful too – just the distant drone of the road traffic and the rhythmic rumble of passing trains pierce the breeze.

The track emerges from the woods into a shallow dip between the pastures of Erringden Grange and Edge End Moor and continues to Lower Rough Head Farm. After climbing a stile beyond the farmhouse, head south-west across a narrow field with a drystone wall to the right.

By now Stoodley Pike's monument is plainly in view, crowning steep moorland slopes. After crossing another stile and continuing to the next wall (at GR977251), turn left (south-east) and climb a ladder

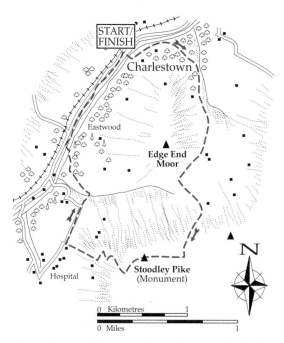

stile to the grandly named London Road, which is more often than not a very muddy cart track.

The climb to the ridge commences on the opposite side of the "road". A good path rakes across moorland slopes past the Doe Stones and a little spring. A stile at a wall corner then precedes the last pull west to the Stoodley Pike's impressive summit, where that grimy 120ft/37m obelisk dominates all.

The monument has a history of collapses. It was first built in 1815 after three locals, Tom Sutcliffe, Sam Greenwood and Bill Ingham were granted permission by the land-

owners to commemorate the Peace of Ghent, and Napoleon's abdication. Their original monument looked like a mill chimney, but it came tumbling down in 1854, on the day the Russian Ambassador left London at the start of the Crimean War. The present monument was constructed in 1856 when that peace was declared. It had a partial collapse in November 1918, just before the end of the First World War.

Those wishing to enter the monument can do so from the northern side. A spiral staircase leads eerily into its darkest recesses to emerge on a viewing platform at the top of the plinth. The twin hamlets of Mankinholes and Lumbutts nestle below on a pastured shelf above the Calder valley, where Todmorden lies, tucked beneath smooth-profiled hills. Across the valley the complex of field, farm and woodland radiate from scattered hillside hamlets, while stone-built and whitewashed weavers' cottages cluster around the church towers of Cross Stone and Heptonstall.

Descend from the monument on a path zigzagging steeply down Stoodley's steep western flanks. Cross the London Road between the new housing estate and the old hospital and turn right along the lane past Middle and High Stoodley Farms. The lane descends to cross a wooded clough before arcing left through Height Woods. A signposted footpath leaves it and delves a little deeper into the woods before following the canal. It switches to the towpath on reaching the bridge at GR968260. Follow the towpath through a mix of woodland and warehouse to Callis Wood, where a left turn along the lane leads quickly past the sewage works to the start of the walk.

30 Langfield Common

This walk on a paved causey track climbs from the valley farms to the high moors of Langfield Common. It is a classic Calderdale walk, on the quiet side of Stoodley Pike. The craggy high point at Coldwell Hill is just 200yds/m from the busy Pennine Way, but the wayfarers only have eyes for the Pike and the route ahead. One by one, they pass by. This route lingers, then descends on another of those causey paths to discover the hill-side village of Lumbutts where it makes a pleasant return across pastureland to the valley.

Distance:
7 ¹/₂ miles/12km

Height gain:
885ft/270m

Walking time:
4-5 hours

Start/Finish:
St. Peter's Gate, Walsden (behind the post office). GR934220.

Type of walk:
A steady but unrelenting climb to the moorland plateau on paved causey tracks and rough, grassy moorland. Good paths along the moorland edge followed by field paths and canal towpath.

Follow St. Peter's Gate across the Rochdale Canal at Travis Mill Lock, climbing with it to North Hollingworth Farm. Keep left in front of the well-maintained whitewashed cottage to follow the signposted Salters Rake bridleway north. The paved track dips into a wet, rushy hollow above Henshaw Wood before climbing out on to the open moor, where there are good views back to Walsden and Ramsden Wood. Leave the track by a cairn at Rake End for an intermittently faint path climbing east across rough grassy slopes. The new path gains confidence as it gains height.

Watch out for the Basin Stone, which lies just to the right of the path. It is a strange gritstone rock that stirs the imagination into conjuring up lions' heads, chefs' hats and all sorts of weird and wonderful things.

The Gaddings dam has been camouflaged by its grassy cloak, but suddenly the walker stumbles across it and climbs the stone staircase to its causeway.

It may not have a good shape, but Gaddings' expansive rectangular waters reflect the moorland skyline to perfection – from Stoodley Pike and its monument, through the serrated craggy top of the Holder Stones, to Blackstone Edge. It is much frequented by birds, too, including winter-visiting whooper swans.

Follow the northern causeways to pass a second reservoir. This one is dry and covered with moorland grasses. Beyond it, the path follows the line of a concrete drain with the Langfield Edge drawing closer from the left. Great gritstone crags overlook some quarries and a network of old miner's tracks climb from the villages of Lumbutts and Mankinholes, which bask in fields below.

The main track beneath the edge, however, is a cotton famine road, built in 1862 by unemployed mill workers. They were laid off during the cotton famine when the American Civil War meant an interruption in the supplies of cotton.

The path traverses some wet, rushy ground as it circumvents a craggy ravine. It continues along the edge, climbing to the north of Jeremy Hill. Keep with the path until you see a huge rock to the right capped by a pile of stones; this is Coldwell Hill.

Coldwell Hill is well worth a detour. From it the Withens Clough Reservoir and Cragg Vale come into view for the first time. They are added to a wide horizon, that includes the Holder Stones and Blackstone Edge, and, of course, Stoodley Pike, which lies across an expanse of moor grass.

Descend north-east from the summit to meet the bold Pennine Way path, which continues along the edge to the pass of Withens Gate. A tall gritstone obelisk, the Long Stoop, marks an old paved corpse road straddling the moors. Here the route joins the Calderdale Way. Turn left along the paved path that zigzags down the hillside towards the three little reservoirs of Lumbutts. Climb the stile to take the left fork, a walled cart track passing the dams towards Lumbutts, temporarily leaving the Calderdale Way (CW), which goes right for the youth hostel at nearby Mankinholes. The track meets a surfaced lane by the Lee Dam, which leads into the village, passing close to the Top Brink Pub for those in need of refreshment.

Lumbutts Tower, on the next corner, completely overshadows the village. It was once part of a cotton mill (long demolished) and contained three vertically-set water wheels fed from above by siphoning water from the four reservoirs.

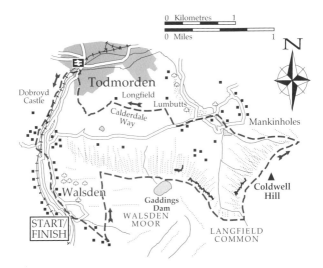

The route rejoins the Calderdale Way along the road past the Causeway Farm complex (not named on the maps) and follows it on a cart track heading north between the cottages of Croft Gate.

Leave the track as it bends left for a field path through a gap stile to the right. The path follows the wall and heads west for Far Longfield, a farming hamlet, scaling several stiles in crosswalls. After turning half right on a lane to pass in front of the last cottage in the group, go through a stile with a CW waymark and head across fields to the nearby Longfield Farm. Pass between the lines of stables and turn left (south) along a walled lane with the crags of the Langfield Edge directly ahead.

Turn right at a T-junction with a surfaced country lane. The stony track now heads north-west with Dobroyd

Castle dominant on the hillsides across the valley. Todmorden soon appears as the path veers to the right with a short stretch of cobbles.

The impressive town hall peeps out between the spire of the Unitarian Church and the railway viaduct.

Beyond a row of terraced cottages the track becomes a Tarmac lane descending steeply past the grimy church, built in 1869 by the town's main benefactors, the Fieldens, in memory of their father. It emerges on the Rochdale road in the centre of Todmorden. Turn left along the busy road and follow it to Dobroyd Road, an unsurfaced lane that climbs over the Rochdale Canal before veering left to a gate by the railway track. Cross with care!

The lane continues its climb through the trees with fleeting glimpses of the town below. It becomes surfaced near the gatehouse of Dobroyd Castle.

Dobroyd Castle is a Victorian mock-Tudor castle built by John Gibson, the architect of the Unitarian church and the town hall, for the Fieldens.

Descend along the road past several stone cottages and cross the A681 Bacup road to gain the canal towpath, which leads the route easily back between mills and cottages to the Travis Mill Lock. Turn right along St. Peters Gate for a return to the starting point.

31 Warland Reservoir Circuit

The Warland Reservoir circuit starts high and stays high, on a heather-clad plateau filled with shallow reservoirs. Well graded supply roads make this the easiest walk in the book, suitable as a late afternoon or evening walk? In twilight as the sun sinks beneath the western hills spreading the pinkish glow of evening, the lights of Greater Manchester twinkle into life through rising mists. The wide view at these times is unforgettable. Be sure to take a torch and allow at least three hours of daylight to get around the moors to the east – the western tracks are no problem in the dark as long as there is moonlight.

Distance:
9 miles/15km

Height gain:
66ft/20m

Walking time:
3 1/2 hours

Start/Finish:
Public car park by the White House Inn. GR968178.

Type of walk:
Easy. Mainly level stony tracks by reservoirs and leats. There are no climbs.

The four major reservoirs of the plateau, Blackstone Edge, White Holme, Lighthazzles, and Warland, were completed in 1804 to keep Rochdale Canal full. The building of the railways signalled a decline in traffic, however, and the reservoirs were sold to the Oldham and Rochdale Corporations for the supply of drinking water. They are now owned by North West Water.

A signpost proclaims the gravelled road along the dam of the Blackstone Edge to be the Pennine Way. It is the easiest section of that famous long distance footpath and leads effortlessly round Cow Head to follow a concrete leat connecting the string of reservoirs.

Views from the outset have been extensive: Pendle Hill is, as ever, a colossus. It dominates the skyline beyond the white windmills of Cliviger, while a line of crags known as Reddyshore Scout overlooks the half-hidden Roche valley. Light Hazzles Edge has some good gritstone rocks and a quarry used by practising climbers. One of the rocks has a perched boulder looking a bit like a wolf's head from some angles.

Abandon the Pennine Way track beyond the quarry at Light Hazzles for a similar stony track to the right (signposted "Reservoir Circuit, White Holme"). It passes along the southern tip of Light Hazzles Reservoir, then bends to the right along the shores of the White Holme Reservoir. Ignore the right fork by the reservoir's southern tip, but instead turn left along the rock-filled dam. Beyond White Holme, the stony track degenerates into a good path through heather, following the line of a concrete leat (the Warland Drain).

The scene has improved. Interesting rocks jut out of the heather slopes of White Holme Moss and the proud

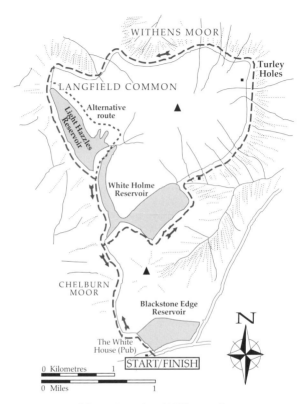

escarpment of Great Manshead Hill soars from a narrow road straddling a wild moorland pass to Mytholmroyd. The acutely-pitched cairn capping the rocks at GR982208 looks as if the first good wind of winter will blow it down, but it has stood for many years now.

As the path turns the corner beyond it, the drain becomes less conspicuous, being overrun by rushes and heather. Suddenly, on Turley Holes and Higher

House Moor, Stoodley Pike comes into view, piercing the skyline. The path swings to the west round the Clove Stones, which are capped by a good cairn. After passing a ruin the drain is replaced by a pipeline with inspection shafts. The path has been obscured by new drainage work, but a few waymarking posts show the line.

Withens Clough Reservoir comes into view on the right, as does an impressive ruin, Red Dykes, on the pastured hillsides above it.

The trig point at Little Holder Stones just beyond the rocks marks the highest summit of this moorland block, including the Pike.

The pipeline changes back to a drain on Birds Nest Hill and the path across grassy moorland becomes clear again. It reacquaints itself with the Pennine Way at a sharp left turn, south of the stony Coldwell Hill. Turn left along it across Langfield Common to the head of the Warland Reservoir. There are rights of way on both sides of the lake. If the rivers and streams are full use the stony track across the western dam, but otherwise cross the drain – strangely no bridge is provided. A narrow path heads for the boulders of Stony Edge on the eastern side, passing a little clapper bridge (do not cross it). Follow the raised grassy causeway round Little Dove Howe. It comes to an abrupt end by a feeder stream close to the eastern extremes of Light Hazzles Reservoir (this end is often empty and unrecognisable as a reservoir).

Cross the stream with care and continue along the raised causeway along the reservoir's north-western shores to rejoin the stony Pennine Way road. Follow it along Light Hazzle's western shores to meet the outward route by the old quarry.

32 Great Manshead Hill

Great Manshead Hill is a fine angular escarpment rising from Cragg Vale and the Ryburn valley. Walkers on the Pennine Way across Blackstone Edge will have noticed its fine lines, but until now it has been an inaccessible, "out of bounds" top. In 1993, Yorkshire Water and the Calderdale council put their heads together and agreed on a permissive path from the A58 by the Baitings Reservoir. When the route is established and the path ingrained on to the moor, the waymarks will be removed, making this a traditional moorland route for the serious walker. The route can be linked with many other paths to form good long distance routes, and though short, makes a good introduction to the Ryburn valley and its surrounding moors.

Distance:
5½ miles/9km

Height gain:
890ft/270m

Walking time:
3-4 hours

Start/Finish:
Ryburn Reservoir Car Park. (GR024187).

Type of walk:
A mixture of moorland paths and farm tracks with a good woodland path round the Ryburn Reservoir.

The Ryburn Reservoir was completed in 1925 to supply water for Wakefield. Its curved dam holds back a maximum of 209 million gallons of water.

A signposted permissive path begins from the north side of the car park and follows the shores of the Ryburn Reservoir through attractive mixed woodland. The fine woodland setting makes this one of the most attractive of the region's reservoirs.

The shoreline path emerges from the thick woodland to pass Beeston Hall Rocks, great chunks of faulted millstone grit capped by heather and surrounded by birch.

Turn left across the footbridge at the far end of the reservoir following the path signposted to Back o' the Height. A series of gritstone steps climb steeply across the fields aiming for the ruin at the top. Turn right here on a track past Higher Wormald Farm to the Back o' the Height road by the 298m spot height.

Turn right along the road, which descends to cross the Baitings Reservoir on a wide viaduct, then left along the main road.

The Baitings Reservoir is a little newer than the Ryburn. The great concrete dam was completed in 1956 to hold up to 775 million gallons of water. It also draws water from Withins Clough Reservoir, Cragg Vale via the Manshead Tunnel.

A permissive path to Manshead Hill begins opposite the roadside car park just 200yds/m along the road. After negotiating a ladder stile, a gap stile and a small footbridge over the stream, the path climbs along the eastern side of Greenwood Clough with the partial ruins of Manshead Farm on the hillside above. It flirts

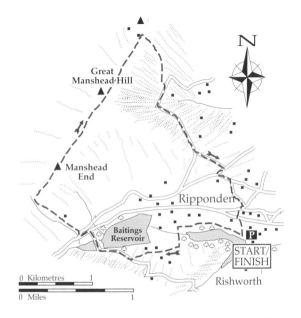

N

Great
Manshead Hill

Manshead
End

Ripponden

Baitings
Reservoir

P

START/
FINISH

0 Kilometres   1

0 Miles   1

Rishworth

with the stream, crossing and recrossing it, before
turning right beyond a stile in the top fence to climb
north-east up the stony slopes of Manshead End.

*The summit is crowned with a concrete trig point and
offers wide views of Stoodley Pike, which lies beyond the
heather and bracken of Turley Holes and Higher House
Moor, and the Warland Reservoirs. To the west, the line of
electricity pylons leads the eye to the crinkled ridge of
Blackstone Edge, while to the south, the view is filled with
the yawning spaces of Rishworth Moor.*

The ridge path wanders through terrain studded with
a few flinty boulders. A little heather mingles with
rough moor grasses and crowberry on the slightly

lower and unmarked top of Great Manshead Hill. The views down Turvin Clough now reveal a few of Cragg Vale's outlying houses peeping out from the heavy woodland cover.

Descending from Great Manshead Hill, the path traverses moorland that is more liberally covered with heather and the inevitable shooting butts appear by the wall encountered above Sykes Farm. On reaching a crossroads of cart tracks turn right, passing an old air raid shelter in the middle of a former quarry. Follow it to the Greave Road (GR012207), a high lane with views down pastoral Blackshaw Clough across the Ryburn valley to Halifax, where the tall and unmistakable profile of the Wainhouse Tower stands proud and clear.

Turn right along the lane and follow it around the rim of Blackshaw Clough. After about 800yds/m (at GR016198), descend along a walled bridleway, the Flight House Road, to the Blue Ball Road (292m spot height). Turn right, then left, on Tarmac lanes to GR022195, where another walled track descends south-south-east to a partially cobbled lane by a cluster of houses.

Turn right on to Hollin Lane. A signposted footpath descends from here to the A58. In summer it will probably be a little overgrown with nettles, a little bramble and lots of rosebay willowherb. The next path is staggered slightly to the left. Flanked on the left by a fence and wall, it descends across fields to meet a track on the top edge of the woodland surrounding the Ryburn Reservoir.

Turn left along the track and first right to return to the car park.

33 Norland Moor

This walk could have started in the depths of the Ryburn valley at Ripponden, but how galling it would be after an hour's toil to be confronted by a moorland car park. Instead this is an easy stroll from one of the lofty car parks, ideal for a balmy evening when the heather blooms glow purple and the late sun's rays flicker through the grasses.

Distance:
4 1/2 miles/7km

Height gain:
525ft/160m

Walking time:
2 hours

Start/Finish:
Turgate Delph Car Park, Norland Moor, by the Moorcock Inn. GR055218.

Type of walk:
An easy circular walk on a lofty but compact heather moor with a short stretch of woodland and a few cross-field farm paths.

Norland Moor's 235-acre gritstone plateau has been popular with the local population since being bought by public subscription in 1932. The quarry at its northern edge was formerly used to extract stone for the Rochdale Canal.

Climb on the deeply-grooved sandy path from the Moorcock Inn over rough grassland and crag to the upland hollow of the old quarry, which is now overgrown with an advancing carpet of heather.

A solitary oak seems to have found a sheltered niche in which to flourish. There are many paths over the moor, but follow the one north-east along the cliff edge. It has views down the deep Ryburn valley to Sowerby, an old village on a pastured hill, and its offspring, Sowerby Bridge, where high rise flats and mill chimneys peep out from the housing estates and shops.

Halifax soon appears, highlighted by the tall Wainhouse Tower, its dark red sandstone always seeming to be in shadow. Completed in 1875, the 253ft (77m) former dye works chimney has 403 steps inside and is occasionally open to the public. It is an excellent viewpoint for both the town and surrounding moors.

After moving away from the edge and past some scrubland, the path goes under a line of pylons and reaches the eastern edge of the moor close to a country lane. Note the fine former clothiers' houses at nearby Norland Town.

The path curves right to pass under the pylons once more by a wall corner. Here five paths meet. Take the south-easterly one to reach the lane at a T-junction. Go straight across on Turbury Lane, crossing the bridge before turning left along a stony track to the north of a farm bungalow. After going through a gate the track continues across fields bordering North Dene Woods, whose upland spread hereabouts is quite thin, allowing plenty of light for a thick carpet of heather and bracken.

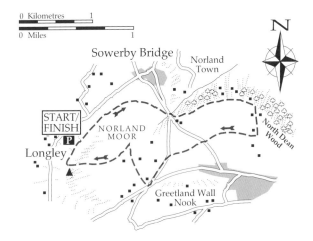

The track degenerates into a path and the woods get thicker with birch and oak; in places the trees spread to the right of the path. After going through a couple of stiles, the path descends a little bank to enter the woods. It keeps close to the top edge of the woodland, with the houses of Halifax flickering through gaps in the trees, and is eventually joined by a cart track from the valley bottom.

Climb out of the woods with this new track, passing the entrance to a small farmhouse before swinging right past another.

Go straight ahead at the crossroads of tracks, but turn right through the gap stile on the waymarked path (at GR083217), just short of the stone-built Moor Bottom Farm. The partially paved path, which is confined by a wall and an electric fence, heads west through several fields with gap stiles in the crosswalls. It emerges on Turbury Lane before continuing opposite across another field – keep the wall to the left. A fenced green lane cuts across the path. After scaling the stiles across it, continue east by the field edge and traverse some scrubland surrounding an old quarry. If it is overgrown with summer shrubs, follow the old quarry tracks to Norland Road, otherwise keep to the edge.

Turn left along the road past a sports ground to the Spring Rock Inn where they grow their own vegetables (a good sign if you want a bar meal). Turn right beyond the pub on a stony track heading north-west towards Spring Head Farm. Home wine-makers will be interested in the bramble and elder that line this bit of the route. At a bend in the track preceding the farmhouse, go through a gap stile to the right and continue north across fields, keeping the wall to the left. After swapping to the left side of the wall at a stile in the second field, the path continues north to the heathlands of Norland Moor.

Turn left on the clear rutted path parallel to an old drystone wall and fence. Another sandy path cuts across the route where the wall veers left. Turn right along this path, heading directly for the white-painted trig point, surrounded by heather and a little gorse. The path continues to Ladstone Rock, a huge crag of millstone grit at the moor's edge.

The Rock is a fine perch overlooking the Ryburn valley. From it the patchwork of walled pasture is laid like a verdant spider's web cast across Crow Hill. Lines of electricity pylons carry their charge, climbing across the moors to straddle the great Pennine watershed at Blackstone Edge.

Turn right to follow the cliff edge path into the hollow of Turgate Delph quarry, where the outward path descends to the car park.

THE MOORS OF MARSDEN, LITTLEBOROUGH AND SADDLEWORTH

South of the Ryburn valley, the Pennines narrow considerably into one pronounced ridge, squeezed by the urban sprawl of Greater Manchester and Huddersfield. The valleys and coombes that cut into the ridge are filled with the conurbation's last outposts. Spartan, but of great character, these Pennine villages of gritstone tuck themselves into niches in the shadow of the dark cotton-grass moors and at the very edge of industry.

Transport has played a big part in the life of these hills, for Man has toiled to build highways that go back many centuries, from the Blackstone Edge Roman road to the 20th-century M62 motorway. He has even burrowed beneath them to build railways and canals, such as those at Standedge. Old drove roads that have almost disappeared into the mosses still lead walkers to the hilltops.

The most northerly peak of the group is Blackstone Edge, called "the English Andes" by writer, Daniel Defoe. Its boulder-strewn summit caps moorland of heather and peat. The southern slopes, Redmires, were once described as the worst mile of the Pennine Way. Wayfarers now have it easy, for recently laid heavyweight gritstone slabs cover much of the path. Typical of this region, the eastern slopes slip into Calderdale in an endless spur clothed in cotton grass and broken only by the waters of Green Withens Reservoir.

The theme continues on Marsden Moor, where the

peatlands end abruptly on the outcrops of Northern Rotcher and Standedge. The little town of Marsden on the Yorkshire side offers superb walks across remote moorland to the tops, saving that view from the western edge to the very last moment.

On the fringes of the Peak District, the rocky edges of Saddleworth provide some of the most spectacular routes in the South Pennines. Dramatic boulder-strewn slopes plummet from the dark crags that fringe the peat moors into the tight ravines of the Chew and Greenfield Brooks, which have long since been flooded by three reservoirs. The firm terrain of the cliff-edge allows fine walking away from the peat line with weird shaped rocks and pillars adding to the appeal of those views over the precipices.

34 Rishworth Moor to Blackstone Edge

What a contrast this walk offers. The first footsteps are round the pretty wooded shoreline of the Ryburn Reservoir, after which the route embarks on a journey through the expansive Rishworth Moor to Blackstone Edge. From this rugged gritstone top the plains of Manchester and Merseyside recede to the pale blue outlines of the North Wales mountains. Pennine Way footpaths carry the route back to Green Withens Reservoir, where the wild moors entertain a yacht club. There is a strange juxtaposition of old and new where the ancient Blackwood Edge path runs parallel to the buzzing M62 motorway.

Distance:
10 miles/16km

Height gain:
1,050ft/370m

Walking time:
5 hours

Start/Finish:
Car park at Ryburn
Reservoir. GR024187.

Type of walk:
High moorland route on
permissive footpaths.

**The route is
waymarked, but not
recommended in mist.**

A signposted permissive path begins from the north side of the car park and follows the shores of the Ryburn Reservoir through attractive mixed woodland. The fine woodland setting makes this one of the most attractive of the region's reservoirs. After leaving the thickest of the woodland behind, the shoreline path skirts the Beeston Hall Rocks – great chunks of faulted millstone grit capped by heather and surrounded by birch.

Turn left across the footbridge at the far end of the reservoir, following the path signposted Back o' the Height. A series of gritstone steps climbs steeply across the fields, aiming for the ruin at the top. Turn right here on a track past Higher Wormald Farm to the Back o' the Height road by the 298m spot height.

Staggered to the left across the road, a signpost points the way "To Blackstone Edge". Go through the gate and along a walled track climbing Grey Stone Height with the Baitings Reservoir visible to the right. The whitewashed inn above it is the Blue Ball, said to be haunted.

Once on the open moor, the old quarry road becomes a twin sunken track through reedy moor – a kind of 19th-century dual carriageway. Gradually it becomes less defined until, in the middle regions across Cat Moss, it degenerates into an intermittent narrow path. Fortunately yellow-capped waymarking posts highlight the line of the route.

At GR994174, the path follows the line of an old drain circumventing Warm Withens Hill. Once round the hill, Blackstone Edge appears, its gritstone boulders topping peaty upper slopes. A signpost pointing backwards ("To the Baitings") marks the intersection with the concrete leat known as the Rishworth Drain. Turn

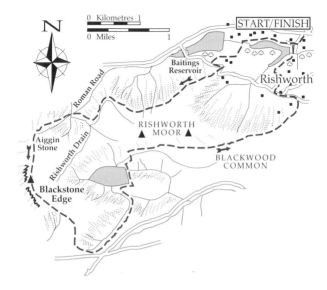

right here following the drain to its intersection with the Blackstone Edge Roman Road, hereabouts named Old Packhorse Road on current maps.

Turn left at the signpost marked "Pennine Way, Blackstone Edge", crossing a footbridge over the leat, to climb on the right hand side of the wide, sunken track filled with reeds and cotton grass. The path, partially paved in its upper reaches, gains the ridge by the Aiggin Stone.

A sandy path climbs south through rocks, heather and cotton grass to the trig point on Blackstone Edge's bouldered summit.

The views across the plains of Manchester, Merseyside and

North Wales are spectacular. On a clear winter's day they will reach to hills of the Peak District, the Clwydians and the peaks of Snowdonia. On nearby Hollingworth Lake sailing boats and windsurfers should be scudding across the water.

Continue south along the edge, then south-east along the Pennine Way route across Redmires. Pathmakers have built numerous cairns and laid a firm stony path across the moors. The yellow stone road makes a bee-line for the GPO mast on Windy Hill to join an old stony track that veers left alongside the M62 motorway. Do not cross on the Pennine Way footbridge but follow the signposted path to Green Withens Reservoir. It descends to a stone-built reservoir leat by a rush-filled trough where dippers play.

A path along the leat is joined by a stony track that leads past the yacht club to the reservoir's dam. Turn right at the northern end of the dam, following another leat-side path marked to Blackwood Edge (ignore those signposted to Blackstone Edge and to Oxygrains). Cross the fourth footbridge along the leat (the third and fifth have little ruined huts by them). A narrow path climbs through bracken. In its upper reaches its course is highlighted by one or two yellow-capped posts. Beyond the boulders of Whinney Nick, the path becomes intermittent and confused by some prominent tracks leading off the fell towards the motorway – be content to follow the line of the posts. At one particularly awkward section watch out for an old cairn that marks the route.

Eventually the path reaches Blackwood Edge on the north side of the ridge. The Baitings and Ryburn reservoirs come into view across a labyrinth of field patterns. Ripponden village lies below, tucked in the twisting, heavily wooded Ryburn valley.

Follow the edge and cross the ladder stile in a tall stone wall. The old road passes a little pond then descends the northern slopes to Pike Law. Turn left at the bottom wall to go through a gate and by the farm to the road and left again along the road to the T-junction.

It is feasible to get back to Ryburn Reservoir by following farm tracks through Upper Cockcroft and Cheetham Laithe, but for a more leisurely route, turn left at the junction, then right along the New Gate track (GR018180). After about 200yds/m, a stile by a gate to the left marks the start of a path down to the reservoir shores.

Confined by a fence and wall, the path can be slightly overgrown in summer. At the bottom of the pastures it turns right to the reservoir shores and transforms into a pleasant path though woodland. To get back to the car park at the start of the walk, cross the huge dam where there are spectacular views to the river-side mills at the bottom of the deep, wooded Ryburn valley.

35 Blackstone Edge

Blackstone Edge, which so impressed writer and traveller Daniel Defoe that he made comparisons with the Andes, stands out from the surrounding peaks: it is a little steeper, a little higher, a little shapelier, but most of all, there are rocks on top. The route from Hollingworth Lake visits an attractive wooded glen, a Roman road and a good way across the rocks to view one of the widest panoramas in the South Pennines. It will be at its best on an afternoon in late spring or early summer when the cottage gardens and woodlands of the lakeside are ablaze with colourful blooms and the descending sun shines obliquely across the crags to highlight the hill's noble form.

Distance:
7 miles/11km

Height gain:
1,000ft/305m

Walking time:
4 hours

Start/Finish:
Hollingworth Lake Car Park, Littleborough.
GR939153.

Type of walk:
A moderate walk on farm tracks, followed by the cobbled Roman Road and good moorland paths.

Hollingworth Lake was built around 1800 to maintain water levels in the Rochdale Canal. Nowadays it is at the heart of an immensely popular country park and nature reserve. From its shores, the serrated gritstone crest of Blackstone Edge climbs to the horizon beyond the rolling flanks of Clegg Moor.

Follow the track from the car park north-east past trees lining the foot of Cleggswood Hill (marked as the Station-to-Station Walk on the South Pennine Leisure map). When the track turns right, abandon it for a flagged path that continues north-east, traversing a field where picnic benches border a little stream and a delightfully situated pond. The path crosses the stream by way of a narrow footbridge, then traces its eastern banks.

Small rounded hills, parcelled by drystone walls, are fringed with deciduous woodland, resplendent with wild flowers.

Turn left along the stony Ealees Lane, encountered beyond a concrete bridge, then double back up some steps that lead to a footpath climbing the grassy hillock behind the whitewashed Lane Foot Cottage (GR945159). The path descends to cross a stream on a wooden footbridge before heading north-east through oakwoods lining the eastern banks. Turn right on a wide waymarked path along the northern edge of the golf course, passing close to Shaw Lane Farm.

Go through a five-bar gate at the termination of the track and veer left on an unsurfaced lane at Lydgate, roughly tracing the north-south line of electricity pylons at the edge of the open fellsides.

At Lydgate the route follows the beginnings of the Blackstone Edge Roman road, which climbs east between a few huddled cottages. Beyond the cottages it is an inconspicuous worn path climbing over rough grassy hillslopes to a point close to the A58 road.

In retrospective views, Hollingworth Lake appears in its entirety, surrounded by grassy knolls and cultivated pastures, dotted with farmhouses. Further north, rising beyond the dwellings of Littleborough, are the barren slopes of Shore Moor. Ahead the busy highway meanders to the horizon over the high moors, while velvet fields rise in gentle curves beneath Blackstone Edge's rocky crest.

As the old road gains height, it becomes more defined and, on approaching the Broad Head Drain, paving slabs of millstone grit appear. Still further uphill it becomes 16ft/5m wide, complete with flags and divided at the centre with a prominent drainage channel.

The road may or may not be Roman, but the flags are almost certainly of medieval origin. The ancient road attains the ridge by an old guidepost known as the Aiggin Stone.

A cairned path climbs south across a terrain of firm peat and heather towards the summit, which is crowned with many curiously-shaped crags and out-crops overlooking its bouldery western flanks.

The crags make excellent perches on which to admire the superb panoramas that have unfolded. The pale and empty moorland declines to Hollingworth Lake and the vast plains of Greater Manchester, which are punctuated by tower blocks and chimneys, fading to the haze of the Snowdonian skyline.

To the north of the summit, across a flat plateau on which four reservoirs have been built, the monument on Stoodley Pike pierces the skyline preceding more distant views over

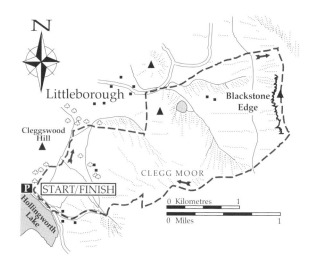

Heptonstall Moor to Boulsworth Hill. Green Withens Reservoir occupies a hollow beneath dull declining moors to the west. It looks at its best in the hazy morning sun, when it appears as a shimmering luminous sheet amongst pallid ethereal hillslopes.

For the descent, follow the line of crags south, ignoring the cairned Pennine Way path, which veers to the left (south-east) towards Redmires. Head south-west from the most southerly crags across the trackless grassy terrain known as Sun End.

Prominent in views ahead at this stage are the GPO's Windy Hill Mast and the bustling M62 trans-Pennine motorway.

At GR969155, by the southern end of Broadhead Drain,

a narrow path commences, tracing the northern edge of Clegg Moor, whose flanks are stony and dark with a mantle of heather. It circumvents a small pool lying in a basin clad with bracken and grass. The pool, curiously named Dry Mere, has plenty of water and did have during the hot summer of 1995.

After passing under a line of pylons, the path meets the Lydgate bridleway at GR954150. Go straight across it along a well-defined path descending rough moors and old quarries to a stony lane that meanders and descends beneath a newly wooded hill and past the cottage of Syke. The lane continues past more cottages to the shores of Hollingworth Lake. It is about 300yds/m south of the car park but, for those who have built up a thirst, 400yds/m from a public house.

36 Oxygrains

The twisting grassy ravine of Oxygrains cuts a deep swath into Rishworth Moor and promises much from the outset. Although close to both the M62 and the A672, within minutes this route reaches the silence of the countryside, where all the speeding will be done by meadow pipits or dippers. The short walk makes a good stroll for a bright summer's evening or when time is short. The extended walk climbs higher along the elusive Blackwood Edge road and takes a more detailed look at the reservoirs of Booth Dean Clough.

SHORT ROUTE:
Distance:
3 miles/5km

Height gain:
245ft/75m

Walking time:
1 1/2-2 hours

Start/Finish:
Oxygrains Bridge.
GR004158. Short
lay-by for car-parking.

EXTENDED ROUTE:
Distance:
5 miles/8km

Height gain:
492ft/150m

Walking time:
2 1/2-3 hours

Type of walk:
A walk over rough
moorland that can be
extended to the moor tops.

**Not recommended in
misty conditions.**

Follow the signposted footpath along a ledge on its southern banks and Oxygrain's promise will soon be fulfilled.

The little path, twisting in and out of the bracken high above the fast-flowing stream, is a delight to walk and discovers some fine gritstone cliffs overlooking the river. They are the Castle Dean rocks and, although the route stays above them, its devious meanderings show them from all angles.

Some well-constructed steps take the path down to ford a side stream north of the rocks, then up again to climb to a wider grassy shelf on the northern banks of Green Withens Clough. The reservoir's grass-covered dam soars above the head of the clough and the path makes a bee-line for its northern corner, passing the outflow to reach the top of the embankment.

Although it is a remote reservoir, Green Withens has its own sailing club – you may see some dinghies sailing across its waters, especially on a Sunday. On the far shore, the moors swell to their craggy zenith on Blackstone Edge. A gentle drone rises from cars and lorries hurrying along the motorway beneath the long and rugged escarpment of Way Stone Edge.

Turn right along the stony causeway road, then right again by the drain traversing Green Withens Moss. The short route follows the drain across rushy moorland beneath Joiner Stones Hill. (The extended route leaves the drain at the fourth bridge across the drain – see below.)

Current maps have the short route's permissive path leaving the drain at GR006164, but the path does not exist and following the map's line would involve an ankle-twisting descent across wet, tussocky moorland.

Instead, stop at the seventh bridge by Castle Dean Springs (GR005165) and follow vehicle wheel tracks downhill: they start south-west but veer south-east to reach the A672 at GR007161.

Cross the road and descend through bracken to turn right along a path tracing the banks of Booth Dean Upper Reservoir, one of four slender lakes. The path is the former course of an old railway used to carry stone for the construction of the Green Withens Reservoir.

By now the grassy corridors of the deep clough shut out the rest of the world, including the motorway. Beyond the reservoir the Oxygrains Old Bridge spans the beck. This fine packhorse bridge precedes the final climb out of the clough to the car.

EXTENDED ROUTE
Leave the water company track at the fourth footbridge along Green Withens eastern drain (GR998168 – the third and fifth have little ruined huts by them),

and climb on a narrow path through bracken. It arcs east and, in its upper reaches, its course is marked by one or two yellow-capped posts. Beyond the boulders of Whinney Nick the path becomes intermittent and confusing with some prominent tracks leading off the fell towards the motorway.

Be content to follow the line of the posts. At one particularly awkward section watch out for an old cairn, which lines the proper route. Eventually the path reaches Blackwood Edge on the north side of the ridge.

The Baitings and Ryburn Reservoirs come into view across a maze of field patterns. Ripponden village appears below, tucked beneath rich pastures in the twisting Ryburn valley.

Follow the edge to a ladder stile in a tall stone wall that straddles the ridge.

Do not cross the stile but turn right on a path that climbs to the brow of the ridge and gradually veers away from the wall. It descends through a gate, then through fields with dilapidated walls. Cross the stile to the left of a barn (Boan Cottage) and continue on its approach road. Turn right at the junction with an unsurfaced lane from Rishworh Lodge. The lane passes through woodland to meet the busy A672 road.

Cross to the other side of the road and descend on a path tracing the shores of the Booth Wood and Booth Dean Reservoirs, passing the Old Oxygrains pack-horse bridge as in the short route and climbing out to the car.

37 Northern Rotcher from Ogden

The Pennines hereabouts are very narrow and confined by the industrial towns of Greater Manchester and West Yorkshire. Climbing to Windy Hill on an old green road, this fine route tracks the Pennine Way on the watershed to view the Tame valley from the rocks of Northern Rotcher. It then flirts with Rapes Highway, an ancient pack-horse trail that would have seen trains of up to forty Galloway ponies carting panniers loaded with wool, coal, lime and cloth.

Distance:
10 miles/16km

Height gain:
1,150ft/350m

Walking time:
5-6 hours

Start/Finish:
Car park by the Ogden Reservoir. GR953123.

Type of walk:
Green roads and moorland paths.

Not suitable for misty conditions.

Ogden is one of a group of reservoirs built between 1858 and 1901 to supply the needs of the Oldham area. The factories beneath its dam are the last vestiges of industry where the town ends and the country begins.

Cross the dam and turn right on a good path with a forest of pine and birch to the left and younger trees on the reservoir banks below. Turn right as the path divides to cross a dyke amid a hollow of bracken, rushes and the odd sycamore tree. The path climbs a grassy bank in a series of steps up, veering left by the ruins of Rachole Farm to meet a prominent cart track at GR952128. Turn left along the track and follow it between the grassy knolls of Dick Hill and Turf Hill to reach a crossroads with the Tunshill Lane path. This is part of the old Rapes Highway, an old packhorse route straddling the Pennines between the Rochdale and Marsden areas.

Turn right along the old highway, which offers a brief glimpse of Hollingworth Lake and the M6 motorway through a gap in the grassy hills. Turn left at a junction beneath the steep slopes of Binns Pasture (some tall gateposts confirm the spot). The new route, a sunken cart track, winds around the hill to climb an undulating spur known as the Windy Hills.

The wall to the left in the early stages is a little too high. Tall people will see over it to confirm that the route runs parallel to the motorway: small people will have to put a spring in their heels to see anything.

If the path is waterlogged, as it often is in the winter months, climb to the rim and follow the well-used drier routes. To the right there are fleeting glimpses of the Piethorne and Norman Hill Reservoirs, while the GPO mast on Windy Hill looks down from the watershed.

The path breaks free of all confining walls on Tag Heys and heads for the mast, rounding it to the left to meet the firm Pennine Way path to the A672 road.

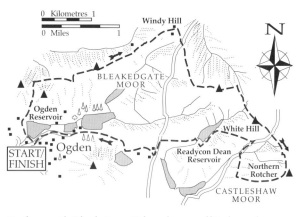

To the north Blackstone Edge shows off its brand new yellow stone path, snaking across Redmires to the summit. You might also see the ubiquitous burger van at the roadside before continuing along the Pennine Way route across the gravel fields of Axletree Edge.

Cairn builders have been active around here; there is plenty of raw material with which to work. The motorway is the dominant feature imparting good symmetry to the scene as it slinks gracefully downhill surrounded by the sleek curves of the moorland escarpments.

The path turns left across peaty ground to head for the trig point on White Hill, where it descends to the head of Readycon Dean. Here the little reservoir peeps out from its tight moorland combe. The National Trust proclaims that this is Marsden Moor and a little stile scales a new fence. A new path and added gritstone steps lead down to slabs across the tiny stream. The new path climbs Rape Hill. More steps and slabs accompany the peat groughs.

It is good to see the little pool on the summit, which can never lose its wide airy views. Pule Hill stands out from the waves of hills that pale to the horizon. Its squat but shapely escarpment fringed with dark crag contrasts with the well-rounded surrounding moors. Behind it, the infamous Black Hill, recognisable by the nearby Holme Moss mast and its slightly darker hue, climbs that bit higher to the skyline, all but blocking out the Dark Peak mires of Bleaklow and Kinder.

Another trans-Pennine road, the A640, appears only at the last minute, lurking in the confines of Haigh Gutter. Once across it, take the right fork (signposted "Pennine Way"). Another improved, park-like path climbs Little Moss to the cairn on Northern Rotcher.

Now Northern Rotcher is a fine viewpoint with gritstone crags forming an edge between the red peaty moors and the pastured valleys. The twin Castleshaw Reservoirs occupy the combe below, with Delph filling a twisted niche between interlocking hills. Amid the complex of tiny roads and tracks by the reservoirs are the remains of a Roman fort. Built for Agricola around AD80, it was strategically sited on the marching route between Chester and York.

The return route follows a waymarked track that forks to the left of the Pennine Way route across Castleshaw Moor: it is marked on the Outdoor Leisure Maps as the Oldham Way. The path starts as a good one, traversing peaty moors. Where the Oldham Way waymarking post turns to the left, continue straight on along a cairned path (this is not the junction with the footpath shown as GR994113 on maps, but about GR997115).

The path narrows and veers right beneath old quarries while the road appears in its deep nick above the Dowry Reservoir. On meeting the A640 road by a footpath signpost, climb uphill for 400yds/m. Turn left along the splendidly firm cart track that skirts the southern slopes of Rapes Hill. It drops to the shores of the Readycon Reservoir, which was spied earlier from the watershed. This is a delightful place with its lake crammed between small, steep-sided and verdant hills. The firm track traces the southern shores and crosses the dam to finish on the A672 road. Turn left downhill for 200yds/m to the Rams Head.

Turn right along the track between the pub and the farm, passing some sheep pens. A waymarking post shows the start of the footpath to the left, which cuts diagonally across a long field to a wooden stile at the far end – keep the farmhouse well to the left. Beyond the stile a sunken grassy track descends to the dam of the Rooden Reservoir, crossing a concrete leat on a footbridge.

After crossing a couple of water company roads, the path continues at the far side of the dam on a reedy track raking to the right across low hill slopes. It veers left, rounding the hill slopes into the valley of the Piethorne, Kitcliffe and Ogden Reservoirs.

Where the path becomes a little obscure, keep to the right of a rushy channel to meet the reservoir road by the stile at GR967124.

Follow the road to the car park, which is less than one mile/1.5km distant.

39 Marsden Moor and Standedge

The dark millstone grit rocks of Standedge fringe the high Pennine moors overlooking the scattered Saddleworth villages, a wild and woolly scene that delighted the poet Amman Wrigley. It is one that is saturated in drama, especially when mist swirls among the rocks and red autumn grasses, and the valley drifts in and out of view. This walk tackles Standedge from Marsden by an old packhorse route. Clear underfoot without ever being eroded, it conjures images of those hard-worked Galloway ponies plodding their way to Lancashire. The Pennine Way forges a passage south to the edge and traverses Black Moss to the Wessenden valley, which channels the route back to Marsden.

Distance:
10 miles/16 km

Height gain:
950ft/290m

Walking time:
6 hours

Start/Finish:
Marsden Railway Station. GR046118. Parking in the village.

Type of walk:
A hard, wild moorland walk.

Not recommended in low cloud or poor conditions.

From the station, the walk ambles along the towpath of the Huddersfield Narrow Canal.

A little red boat often chugs past, ferrying passengers on pleasure trips to the cafe, and tourist information shop at Tunnel End, where the watercourse goes subterranean. The 23-mile canal, built by the famous engineer, Thomas Telford in the 1800s, stretches from Huddersfield to the Ashton Canal in Manchester. Its tunnel, burrowing through the Pennine rock, is the longest at a little over 3 miles/5km, and conveys the highest section of canal in the country. As there was no towpath the horses would have to be unhitched, while the boatmen would lie on their backs and propel the boat with their feet. This would take about four hours of hard labour. Meanwhile, the horses would be led to Standedge via the Boat Lane.

In 1950, the lock gates were removed and the waterway beneath the Pennines closed.

Cross the bridge near the tunnel entrance and turn right along the lane that climbs to the Tunnel End Inn. Turn left here and follow the country lane to Hey Green. A footpath, signposted to Willykay Clough, descends through a tree-shaded bower with a babbling stream to the left. Cross the delightful one-arched stone-built Close Gate bridge and take the footpath to the right into the tight twisting gorge of Haigh Clough. Shortly the well-defined footpath swings left beneath a steep-sided grassy knoll to trace the northern banks of Stonepit Lea Clough (note the map has the path steeply climbing the knoll). Stay with it across the grassy moorland to ford Willykay Clough near Stack End. When the moors are wet there is a little waterfall here.

The path climbs parallel to the clough with the March Haigh Reservoir appearing from its hollow to the north. Dominating the high hillside above it, the large and isolated Buckstones House was the scene of an unsolved double murder in 1903.

Above the rushy water leat, the clough changes its name to Oldgate Clough and veers away from the route, which fords Willmer Green Clough, a more substantial watercourse that cuts a little shaly gorge through the hillsides. The old packhorse road now rakes up the slopes of Broad Wham to its modern counterpart, the A640 trans-Pennine road.

Turn left here along the gravelly Pennine Way path that heads south-east along the main watershed. It curves to the left to a cairn beneath Northern Rotcher, where peat comes to the surface in large patches between the grassy moorland and the stony edge. The path to Northern Rotcher's gritstone rocks follows the edge, high above the Castleshaw reservoirs, which occupy a pastured hollow cradled by moorland spurs.

In views to the west, the village of Delph squeezes between low hills in the Upper Tame valley and the earthwork remains of a Roman fort lie close to the upper Castleshaw dam. The fort, built for Agricola around AD80, protected the marching route between Chester and York.

Continue along the gritstone rim to Standedge, where the boulders are of gigantic proportions. Climbers often practise on the old quarried cliffs below the summit trig point. There is also a memorial to Ammon Wrigley (1861-1946), the poet from Delph who often walked these moors, which were frequently the subject of his writings.

Descend on the obvious path from the trig point, scaling a couple of stiles in the crosswalls and fences. Diggle comes into view in its niche beneath the wind-

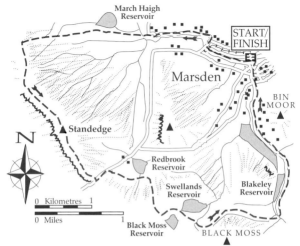

swept Broadstone Hill and Harrop Edge. After crossing a stile over a new fence, turn left along a cart track to the busy road at Standedge Cutting. Take care on crossing because the hill to the left makes pedestrians invisible to cars until the last minute.

The route continues along the Pennine Way to the left of the small car park.

This is the course of another old packhorse road, traversing the moorlands south of Redbrook Reservoir. The reservoir, along with Black Moss and Swellands Reservoir, was constructed to feed the Huddersfield Narrow Canal, which hereabouts burrows beneath the Pennine moors. On a summer Sunday afternoon sailing dinghies will be gliding across Redbrook Reservoir, seldom short of wind.

The Pennine Way route to be followed turns right off the old packhorse road by the breach in its course – some steps mark the spot. The path that climbs to the

Black Moss Reservoir has been paved with massive slabs of gritstone – a little piece of the city here on the moors.

After crossing the reservoir dam, turn left, still on the Pennine Way (Wessenden Loop). The path now is unsurfaced (this may change) and the outlook improves. The Swellands Reservoir appears to the north, then a rushy depression to the south. The latter deepens into the bracken-filled Blakeley Clough into which the path eventually descends to cross the stream by a water intake. The Wessenden valley will have come into view with the large Wessenden Lodge sitting in high fields above the reservoir.

After climbing out of the clough to a grassy spur on the opposite banks, the narrow path dives steeply from the left hand side of an inspection cover into the main Wessenden valley. In retrospective views, some waterfalls cascade down the clough behind a healthy-looking rowan tree.

Cross the river on a little footbridge and turn left along a grassy track. Almost immediately a steep grassy path rakes up the hill to the right to meet the stony reservoir road that runs the length of the valley. Follow it north past the Blakeley and Butterley Reservoirs to Binn Road. En route there is an interesting still life sculpture by Joss Smith, serving as a Kirklees Way footpath waymarker.

Follow the road down into Marsden, keeping straight on to pass beneath the main road and by the church to the railway station.

39 The Station to Station Walk

The Station to Station Walk is an adaptation of the Rapes Highway, a packhorse route from Rochdale to Marsden. The station link is a little odd in that they are on different lines. It is a fine route and one that has the walker following in the hoofprints of the Galloway ponies from Lancashire and Yorkshire.

FROM LITTLEBOROUGH:

Distance:
10 miles/16km

Height gain:
1,245ft/380m

Walking time:
6-7 hours

Start:
Littleborough or Newhey railway stations at GR939163 or GR938116, respectively.

Finish:
Marsden railway station. GR046118.

FROM NEWHEY:

Distance:
8¾ miles/14 km

Height gain:
1,230ft/375m

Walking time:
5½-6 hours

Type of walk:
A moderate moorland walk across the watershed, between the railway stations of Littleborough and Marsden with an alternative from Newhey. It is mostly on cart tracks although the descent to Marsden follows tracks across open moorland.

Public Transport:
It sounds simple, being an official station to station foot-
path, but the stations are not on the same railway line!

Railways:
Halifax to Manchester Victoria stops at Littleborough
and Newhey (Oldham branch line – no Sunday
service). On Mondays to Saturdays trains run from
Manchester Victoria to Marsden, but on Sundays the
Huddersfield-Manchester Piccadilly (no Victoria
service) trains do not stop at Marsden. There is a
service from Marsden to Huddersfield.

Bus:
Halifax to Huddersfield (502, 503, 504): Marsden to
Huddersfield (352) – both regular.

FROM LITTLEBOROUGH:
From Littleborough Station take the A58 Halifax road
under the railway bridge and past the Red Lion pub.
Turn right along Ealees Road past some terraces and
Ealees Mill. The aspects become more rural beyond
the gate at Old Mill Cottage, where the road becomes
a stony lane delving into a sylvan glade between two
hills.

The lane curves to the right beneath Ealees Wood,
then sharp left towards Lane Foot. At this second bend
turn right to follow a signposted footpath across a
concrete bridge. Beyond a gate the pleasant path
traces the stream beneath Clegg Wood.

Looking to the horizon the dark crinkled summit of
Blackstone Edge towers above the cluster of cottages
at Whittaker. Cross the stream on a wooden footbridge

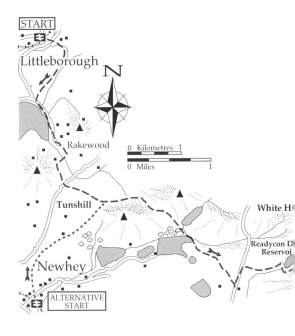

and continue along the opposite banks. Turn half right on a paved path by picnic tables and a charming little pond. The path meets a tree-lined track, passing the Hollingworth Lake Visitor Centre and terminating at the lakeshore road.

Hollingworth Lake was built around 1800 to maintain water levels in the Rochdale trans-Pennine canal, which was opened four years later. The subsequent building of the Manchester to Leeds railway in 1841 led to the prosperity of this cotton weaving and spinning area. Local weavers who could not afford a trip to the seaside would come to Hollingworth Lake in great numbers. It came to be known as the 'Weighvers Seaport' and all the trappings of a Victorian resort were added - hotels, promenades, gardens and pleasure trips on lake steamers.

Turn left along the promenade heading south to the old mill and weavers' cottages at Rakewood, then right across a stream to the grounds of Littleborough Rugby Club. The marked path along Deep Lane is choked with nettles and is impassable. It is advisable to pass along the northern and western edges of the rugby grounds to the gap stile in the fence at the far end.

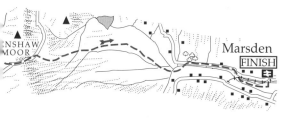

Take the left fork at the foot of Castle Hill. The path skirts the eastern side of the little knoll to pass through the little valley of Langden End Brook and between the great concrete pillars beneath the motorway viaduct. The valley curves east and there is a fork in the paths. Take the right one, which climbs across the lower slopes of Dick Hill, where there are splendid views back to the lake. Go over the steel ladder stile on the shoulder of the hill and cross a stony cart track to scale an identical stile.

On the other side is the Tunshill Lane path where the Newhey alternative route is joined. This sunken grassy lane climbs between stone walls, as it has done for centuries. Take the right fork by some tall gate-posts beneath Binns Pasture (GR961134) and descend to the eastern shores of the Piethorne Reservoir beneath the dam of the higher Norman Hill Reservoir. The track now climbs south-east on a moorland spur above Cold Greave Clough. It crosses a drain from the Rooden Reservoir before reaching the busy A672 road by the Rams Head pub.

Turn left up the road for 300yds/m, then right on a stony track into Readycon Dean. The reservoir here is strangely attractive, occupying a tight valley surrounded by steep-sided grassy hills. The track crosses the dam and continues along the southern shores before climbing out of the dean to another trans-Pennine road, the A640. The walk has now reached the 400m contour and the setting is one of high moorland. Turn left along the road to the main Pennine watershed by Haigh Gutter.

Ignore the Pennine Way path and take the left fork, which is paved for a short way. This old packhorse route descends a little escarpment into the Willmer Green Clough, which it fords at GR011124. The occasional concrete posts inscribed with the letters PH (pack horse) confirms the line, but the path is clear under foot. The angular gritstone-fringed Pule Hill dominates the view ahead, largely because its character contrasts with the surrounding rounded hills. Gradually the path veers south-east and fords Willykay Clough by some little waterfalls at Stack End.

Now a narrow path, it descends to the impressive Close Gate packhorse bridge that spans the infant

River Colne. Turn left beyond the bridge, climbing a tree-shaded path to a country lane by Hey Green. Follow the lane east to the Tunnel End Inn where a lane leads downhill to the canal side at Tunnel End where there is a tourist information centre, shop and cafe. Here the Huddersfield Narrow Canal disappears into the dark recesses of the Pennines to emerge on the western side at Diggle.

The Station to Station Walk finishes on an easy note, following the canal towpath for 800yds/m to the metro station at Marsden.

FROM NEWHEY:
The Newhey alternative is probably the finer of the two routes. It gets to grips with the hills much earlier and spends little time on Tarmac. Climb some steps on the opposite side of the road to the station and turn left on a cobbled lane that climbs past Newhey's spired church. Turn right on the cart track that threads between the cottages of Bradley before heading north on the pastured sides of Moy Hill.

Take the left fork, a grassy track that circumvents the lower slopes of the hill to pass through the rubble of a ruined farm building before descending to the cobbled Carr Lane. Cross a stile and turn right along the rough stony lane past the cluster of cottages and warehouses of Newfield Head. Shaded by trees for a while, it climbs parallel to the motorway, past Carr Farm. Turn right at the T-junction beneath Dick Hill. The new track, Tunshill Lane, climbs gently up the hillside. The Piethorne Reservoirs appear below in pleasant southern views that are complemented by the stony flanks of Great Hoar Edge. The walled track meets the Littleborough route by a metal ladder stile at GR952134 between Dick Hill and Town Hill.

40 Saddleworth Edges

The Saddleworth Edges form the most southerly extremes of the South Pennines, lying at the edge of the Peak District National Park. They are popular with walkers, who flock here at weekends to climb to the rocky edges. Somehow the cliff-tops are more appealing than the high moorland summits hereabouts, where the infamous Black Hill lies waiting. This circuit explores the southern edges above Dove Stone Reservoir and sneaks across the Peak District border for a look at Laddow Rocks and the Pennine Way.

Distance:
9 miles/15km

Height gain:
1,210ft/370m

Walking time:
5 hours

Start/Finish:
Binn Green Car Park.
GR018044.

Type of walk:
A rough moorland walk using a combination of forest paths, both stony and peaty moorland paths, and water company roads.

Map: OS Dark Peak Outdoor Leisure Map.

Head south-west down the lane at the bottom of the car park and, close to its exit at the main road, turn left to descend the path through the woods.

Turn right along a path parallel with Dove Stone Reservoir's shores.

The reservoirs of the valley were built at different times: Yeoman Hey (1880), Greenfield (1902) and Dove Stone (1967). They are set spectacularly amid the wild, sullen-cragged ravines of the Chew and Greenfield Brooks.

Go through the Dove Stone Car Park and turn right along Bradbury's Lane, passing New Barn, a large loomhouse. Turn left opposite the 19th-century terraced mill cottages of Hey Top through a gap in the wall and over a stile to climb the hillside ahead on the west bank of a stream. On entering the pine plantation cross to the east banks of the stream then turn left along a narrow path, Intake Lane.

Beyond a gate at the forest's edge, the path continues across boulder-strewn slopes to ford a stream by some stepping stones before entering the Chew Piece Plantation, a pleasing mix of sycamore, oak, rowan and ash. Through the trees the hillsides swell to the craggy fringe of Wimberry Stones Brow and the views of the Chew valley's craggy inner sanctum gradually unfold.

After climbing a wooden stile at the far edge of Chew Piece, follow the path east across Rams Clough, heading into Chew Brook's tightening ravine. Some steps lead the path down to cross the brook on a footbridge before it climbs the far banks to Chew Reservoir's supply road.

As the cliffs converge to shut out the skies, this Tarmac road climbs steadily to the shoulder of the moor and the Chew dam.

Chew, which at 1,607ft/490m, is England's highest

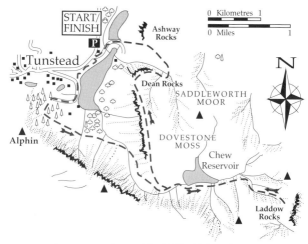

reservoir, was constructed in 1912. Although remote, it is seldom deserted, being a popular weekend picnic site.

Continue along the reservoir's southern shores on the course of an old railway built to supply men and materials for its construction.

The route continues east on a reasonably firm, well-defined peaty path across the peat-hagged expanses of Laddow Moss to emerge on the Pennine Way path at Laddow Rocks. These popular gritstone cliffs overlook the deep ravine of Crowden Great Brook. Most walkers will be heading north for the infamous quagmires of Black Hill, which looks from this vantage no more than a grassy escarpment – appearances can be deceptive!

The route has already strayed into the Peak District hereabouts (that is another book), and so return to the reservoir and its supply road. Abandon the road just short of a disused quarry (GR034017) for a sketchy track heading west. Trace the firmer ground near to the edge, passing numerous strangely-shaped boulders, including the mushroom-shaped Dish Stone, perched high above the deepening Chew valley.

Soon the Dove Stone Reservoir comes back into view. Beyond it is Alderman Hill, topped by a gritstone-bouldered cap and obelisk. The view opens out to reveal more of the reservoir and the verdant surroundings of the mills and dwellings of Greenfield.

The path continues past Bramley's Cot, a rather unusual former shooting hut, built into a cliff edge – the groove can still be seen where the roof would have been attached. A short distance to the north the path passes the cairn on Fox Stone, a memorial to two young climbers killed in the Dolomites in 1972.

The route now enters the finest stretch of crag scenery of the day. The Great Dove Stone Rocks fringe boulder-strewn flanks, which tumble to the reservoir below. Another reservoir, the Yeoman Hey, is now in view to the north, flanked by a small plantation of conifers, lending a little fresh colour to the scene.

Beyond the Great Dove Stone rocks, the path veers right (east) to cross the Ashway Gap. It is quite a circuitous but unavoidable detour. Ford Dove Stone Clough at GR032038 by a small cataract where the path continues at the edge of the moorland to the west of the Ashway Stone.

Ahead are the serrated Ashway Rocks and a cross commemorating the death of MP, James Platt, killed in a shooting accident in 1857. Platt's brother used to own Ashway Gap House, a Victorian castellated mansion and well-known landmark, which stood at the foot of Dovestone Clough until it was demolished by the old water authority in the 1960s.

A well-defined track abandons the plateau's edge and descends beneath the Ashway Rocks. The right of way is shown as zigzagging down to the weirs at the clough bottom but in reality a clear track continues along the grassy flanks to the Water Company road close to the Yeoman Hey Dam. Cross the dam and turn left along the road through conifer plantations, then right following the signposted path back to the Binn Green Car Park.

LONG DISTANCE FOOTPATHS
An Overview

An interesting way to discover the joys of South Pennine walking is to try one of its many long distance routes. Here is a list of the better known official routes, all of which will be waymarked. Most of the guidebooks and leaflets are available from local tourist information centres.

THE BRONTË WAY
A recently extended route connecting places associated with the Brontë family. It is a good route, sampling in equal parts the wild heather moorland, and a wealth of industrial and literary heritage.
Start: Gawthorpe Hall, Padiham. GR SD805340.
Finish: Oakwell Hall, between Bradford and Batley. GR SE217271.
Distance: 40 miles/64km.
Time: 2-3 days.
Route: Gawthorpe Hall, Burnley, Thursden valley, Wycoller, Top Withins, Haworth, Oxenhope, Thornton Moor, Thornton, Norwood Green, Spen valley, Oakwell Hall,
Publications: *The Brontë Way* series of colour leaflets (Lancashire County Planning Department). £1.95.

THE BURNLEY WAY
A circuitous series of loops illustrating how much good scenery exists around the boundaries of Burnley.
Start/Finish: Weavers' Triangle, Burnley.
GR SD838329.
Distance: 40 miles/64km.

Time 2-3 days.
Route: Widdop, Hurstwood Reservoir, Thieveley Pike, Clowbridge Reservoir, Hapton, and Padiham.
Publications: *The Burnley Way*: 5-page leaflet (Burnley Borough Council). Free.

THE CALDERDALE WAY

One of the pioneering long distance routes, this one weaves through the valleys, woods and hillsides of Calderdale giving bird's-eye views of the towns from a rural aspect. It is well worth doing.
Start/Finish: Clay House, West Vale, Halifax.
GR SE097214.
Distance: 50 miles/80km.
Time: 2-4 days.
Route: Clay House, Norland Moor, Ripponden, Mill Bank, Cragg Vale, Mankinholes, Todmorden, Blackshaw Head, Heptonstall, Midgehole, Pecket Well, Luddenden Dean, Brockholes, Illingworth, Norwood Green, Brighouse, Clay House.
Publications: *The Calderdale Way*: 56 page booklet (The Calderdale Way Association). £2.00.

THE KIRKLEES WAY

Visit some of the well-known places from *Last of the Summer Wine* in this Yorkshire circuit around the boundaries of the Kirklees district.
Start/Finish: Scholes. GR SE167259.
Distance: 73 miles/116km.
Time: 3-5 days.
Route: Scholes, Spen valley, Oakwell Hall, Dewsbury, Clayton West, Holme valley, Marsden, Scammonden Reservoir, north of Huddersfield, Scholes.
Publications: *The Kirklees Way* (folder): (Kirklees Metropolitan Council). £6.50 plus 75p postage.

THE OLDHAM WAY

A varied and interesting circular walk showing just how lucky the folk of Oldham are to be so near so many good hills.

Start/Finish: Dove Stone Reservoir. GR SE002036.

Distance: 40 miles/64km.

Time: 2-3 days.

Route: Dove Stone Reservoir, Saddleworth Moor, Pots and Pans, Diggle, Castleshaw Moor, Denshaw, outskirts of Shaw and Royton, Chadderton Hall Park, Rochdale Canal, Failsworth, Medlock valley, Daisy Nook, Hartshead Pike, Quick, Dove Stone Reservoir.

Publications: *The Oldham Way*: 7-page A4 leaflet (Oldham Metropolitan District Council). Free.

THE PENDLE WAY

The Pendle Way is a varied and interesting walk covering both the moorland and rolling pastures of the Pendle witch country. The high point of the final day is a climb to the top of Pendle Hill.

Start/Finish: The Pendle Heritage Centre.

GR SD863398.

Distance: 45 miles/72km.

Time: 2-3 days.

Route: Barrowford, Barnoldswick, Thornton-in-Craven, Wycoller, Reedley, Higham, Newchurch-in-Pendle, Pendle Hill, Barley, Barrowford.

Publications: *The Pendle Way* (pack of 9 leaflets): (Pendle Borough Council). £2.50 plus 50p postage.

THE ROSSENDALE WAY

Discover Lancashire's cotton country on this border circuit of Rossendale. It starts and stays fairly high and would not be suitable for the inexperienced walker in unsettled weather conditions.

Start/Finish: Sharneyford. GR SD889246.

Distance: 45 miles/72km.

Time: 2-3 days.

Route: Sharneyford, Freeholds Top, Hades Hill, Healey Dell, Rooley Moor, Cowpe Moss, Irwell valley, Musbury Heights, Haslingden Grane, Rising Bridge, Love Clough, Sharneyford.

Publications: *Rossendale Rambles* by Ian Goldthorpe (Rossendale Groundwork Trust). 160 page book. £3.75.

Acknowledgements

I would like to thank those who have helped me with the publication of this book: Lowe Alpine of Tullamore, Ireland, for the supply of clothing that kept me safe and warm on the hills; David Norcliffe, of Calderdale Leisure Services for his advice; my wife, Nicola, for her support and for her company on many of the walks, and all the anonymous writers who provided information in the form of tourist leaflets.

This book has been compiled in accordance with the Guidelines for the Writers of Path Guides published by the Outdoor Writers' Guild.

By the same author
Snowdonia to Gower
Bowland and the South Pennines
Peaks of the Yorkshire Dales
The Bowland-Dales Traverse
Pennine Ways
Lakeland to Lindisfarne

INDEX

Printed by Hubbard Print, Dronfield, near Sheffield